THE TOOTSIE ROLL MARINES

A U.S. Marines' memories and letters during the Korean war in 1950 at the Chosin Reservoir.

KEN SANTOR

Fulton Books
Meadville, PA

Published by Fulton Books 2024

ISBN 979-8-88982-860-0 (paperback)
ISBN 979-8-88982-862-4 (hardcover)
ISBN 979-8-88982-861-7 (digital)

Printed in the United States of America

CONTENTS

This book is dedicated to my wife, Anne; Ellen Gordon and the Tootsie Roll Company; and most of all to my fellow Marines that did not make it home. The blessings sent from God to his Marines in the form of the Tootsie Roll candies that we received during the battle of the Chosin Reservoir literally saved the lives of the First Marine Division.

CHAPTER 1

BUFFALO, NEW YORK

On January 14, 1931, at 0800 Eastern Standard Time, I was brought into this world, the fourth son, second generation FBI (full-blooded Italian) bearing the Santor name. It seemed that on this early morning in January, when my father was at work, that God decided he could not wait any longer for me to start my journey on this earth. I was born in a taxicab outside of the hospital, and I guess that my destiny was already set for what I had to do.

When I was four years old, I snuck out of the house to visit my friend who lived down the block. This created quite a panic when my family discovered that I was nowhere in the house. My older brother Albert remembered that a friend of mine was in a house down the street, and he came to fetch me. The parents of my friend told my brother that their little son had scarlet fever, and they said that I had been exposed to it. My parents rushed me to the hospital, and sure enough, I had scarlet fever. I don't remember how long I was in the hospital, but it was pretty bad. In fact, I almost died from it. I do remember that all the nurses on my floor threw me a going-away party when it was over, and they gave me the biggest dish of ice cream that I gulped down and got the biggest headache.

Our family kept on growing, and in 1933, my mother gave birth to a set of twin girls named Aileen and Elaine. In 1935, she gave birth to my little sister named Elizabeth. We now had a total of three boys and three girls.

When I was five years old, my mother's stepbrothers came to live with us. It was Uncle Mike and Frank and Tony Arpaia. My mother's last name was Graganella, as her mother had remarried a man named Arpaia after her husband died. This man had three sons and two daughters, and the daughters' names were Mary and Rose. My mother had two sisters, and their names were Josephine and Florence Graganella. The three boys were placed in a Roman Catholic orphanage until the age of eighteen. It was then that my father took them in. Later, Uncle Mike joined the navy, and Uncle Frank and Tony continued to live with us.

I do remember back then that times were bad. In fact, I remember a time when my two older brothers pulled me on a sled to the Army National Guard Armory to pick up dried fruit, cornmeal, flour, and whatever else they were giving to needy families. We were fortunate that the butcher gave away liver and soup bones because there were lots of mouths to feed.

When I was six years old, I remember my oldest brother Albert coming to our school to pick up Richard and me. He said that our mother was in the hospital, and she wanted to see her family. So there we all were at the hospital, including my twin sisters and little Elizabeth. We were not allowed in to see her because we were too young. Much later, Albert came in and said that our mother had passed away.

Back in those days, it was customary that funerals were held in people's homes, and I remember all the flowers and the friends and relatives who came to pay their last respects. I remember that we were all given a small piece of our mother's dress, which I kept for many years. We did not attend the burial of our mother because of our young age.

Not long after our mother died, our father hurt his back at work and was told that he had to go to the hospital for back surgery. This was really a blow to him, and he was worried about who would watch his children. At this time in 1937, we were just coming out of the Great Depression and times were still pretty rough. People were short of money and other things, and many had just started to go back to work again. My father asked all our relatives for help to take care of our family so we would not be broken up. It was only my father's older sister, Angeline, who lived in Niagara Falls, Canada, that came forward to say that she would take Elizabeth to live with her, since Elizabeth was only twenty-some months old. The rest of us were placed in a Roman Catholic orphanage home. Our father checked us into the orphanage, and I was placed on the first floor. Richard was placed on the second floor, and Albert, who was the eldest, was placed on the third floor. Our twin sisters, Elaine and Aileen, were taken to another building that was for girls only.

There was a time that I had an idea to sneak away to see my sisters. They were in a building on the other side of our playground, and they were really surprised to see me. After a very short visit, I had to get back to my building. All this had happened while there was a big bandage that covered my left eye due to a stye. Mrs. Burgasser, the orphanage nurse, had taped me up and it turned out that she left it there for over thirty days, and I became cross-eyed in my left eye so I saw everything double. One day I was outside playing and running fast and saw that the basketball court had two big poles. Now from memory, I knew that one was not there, so I decided to run through the real one. When I woke up, I was in the nurse's office and got quite a scolding from her. My father came to visit, and when he saw the bandage on my left eye, he went right to the nurse's office and demanded that she remove it. Because the patch had been on for so long, I had to wear glasses for over two years just to straighten out my eyesight.

I remember another time at the orphanage when I was about six years old, and I was placed on the first floor with about fifty other boys. We slept in a very large room with our beds about three feet apart. We were told that after the lights were out, we were never to leave our beds. This created a very nervous situation. If we had to relieve ourselves at night, we would just do it in our beds. My oldest brother Albert had to clean up the mess since he was the eldest of the boys. He teased me for many years after this, saying that I was a bedwetter and reminding me about how he had to clean and replace my bedding every day.

I recall that when the lights were turned off, most of the children in our room would cry for their mothers until they fell asleep. We were told not to leave our beds, but we were afraid of the dark and the strange noises that we heard all night long. To this day, I believe that the building was haunted by the boys that had died in their sleep, or those that died because of sickness. It was a very long time after we left that I would still hear noises and children crying at night.

It seemed that every morning, on our way to breakfast, we would pass a bed with a small child that had died during the night, and the nuns would make us look at the dead body. I was so glad when we finally left this terrible place, and we hoped that we would never ever see it again. Every morning, we would have the same thing for breakfast, which was some kind of hot cereal, an apple, and a cup of hot Postum, which was a drink made from a powdered substance that had a very distinct and memorable flavor. On Sundays we would get the treat of a cinnamon roll along with the cereal, and this is something I really looked forward to; in fact, to this day, I still love cinnamon rolls.

Over the time of our stay there, I saw my sisters and brothers only two times. That was when my father's older sister Mary and Uncle Louie came to visit. I remember this because they brought a large bag of oranges. The second time was when my father came with a strange lady who was a friend of our family. Her name was Mary. The next time when our father came to visit with this lady named Mary, we were told they were married and that we would be leaving this place in a few weeks, or as soon as they could find a place large enough so that we would all be together again as a family. That would include our little sister Elizabeth. After almost three years at the orphanage, we would be together again.

Dormitory at the German Roman Catholic Orphan Asylum, Buffalo New York (above). School, dormitories and chapel (below). https://pbase.com/kjosker/germanorphanasylum&page=all

Western dormitory staircase.

Dining room corridor.

Orphanage kitchen. (https://pbase.com/kjosker/
image/102429213https://pbase.com/kjosker/)

The Santor Family

Albert Carmen Santor was the oldest son. He was born on September 17,1924. He married and had four children, three sons and one daughter. Albert is no longer with us.

Joseph Santor died at birth in June of 1927.

Richard Victor Santor was born on May 16, 1928. He married and had two sons and one daughter, and his wife Nancy passed away.

I was born Kenneth Francis Joseph Santor on January 14, 1931, and married Anne on June 29, 1957. Ken Junior was born on August 13, 1958, and Suzanne was born on April 17, 1963. Anne died in 1981 and Ken Jr. died in 2015. Suzanne has one son and one daughter, and she currently lives in Reno.

Aileen and Elaine (twins) were born on March 6, 1933. Aileen had three sons and one daughter, and Elaine had two sons and four daughters.

Elizabeth Jane Santor was born December 9, 1934, and she married and had one son and one daughter.

James Thomas Santor was born September 15, 1941. He married and had three sons and one daughter, and he currently lives in Henderson, Nevada.

Daniel Santor was born May 3, 1943, and he married Lana, and they had four daughters. Lana passed away, and Daniel currently lives in Sylmar, California.

Louis James Santor was born on September 1, 1945, married, and had three sons and one daughter. One son died. Louis is married and currently lives in Simi, California.

In all, the Santor Family had a total of sixteen boys and fifteen girls. The total number of the Santor family that is still living includes nine boys and ten girls, with all the boys carrying the name of Santor, so truly the Santor name will carry on for some time.

CHAPTER 2

TOGETHER AGAIN

The day came for us to leave the orphanage, and we were so happy that we didn't have to stay any longer. We traveled to our new home where Albert, Richard, and me shared one bedroom, the twins and Elizabeth shared the second bedroom, and my father and his new wife shared the last bedroom. Our new mother was from a family of four boys and four girls. Their father had passed away and the mother never remarried, and the older boys supported the family. Now we had a second family, and Grandma Manzella was a very devout Catholic, going to Mass every morning and of course every Sunday. Grandma would invite us to Sunday dinner, and she was a great cook, except for her cold spinach pie which was terrible. Our dad said to "eat it and shut up" and that's exactly what we did.

When World War II came along, three of the boys joined the army and one joined the navy. They all served in the European sector, and they all returned home without a scratch. Grandma Manzella was so happy, she said that God gave her this for her being so good.

We were all settled in our new home, all of us. It was hard at first, seeing that we had been separated for over three years. It took some time getting used to having brothers and sisters again, along with a new mom. She worked very hard trying to get used to her new family of three boys and three girls, from the ages of sixteen years down to two years, and she did one hell of a job. When my mother had died, I didn't remember too much about her because I was very young, so our new mother was who I considered my real mother.

Life was going pretty well because we had a home and a good Catholic school to go to. Our father had a job where he was earning a little more than $40 a week, and we always had a good meal and would enjoy dinner together every night. One strict rule in our home was that we had to be at the dinner table at six o'clock sharp or no dinner. We all ate the same food, and it was nothing fancy but very nutritional. Sometimes on special occasions we would have home-made bread pudding, made from scraps of homemade bread. Our special meal was on Sunday when we had baked rabbit or chicken. My job was to take care of and feed our chickens. This was some-thing my father and I did together, and he taught me how to build a chicken coop and raise our own chickens from eggs. I even learned how to kill them when it was time, when they were going to be for our meals. I had thirty-six chickens, and it was my job to feed them and collect the eggs. One day he said we were going to try something new, and it was to save all our potato peels and cook them until they were soft, then we would add red chili pepper and feed them to the chickens. Wow, we were now getting thirty-six to thirty-seven eggs a day! We had more eggs than we could eat, and I started to sell them to our neighbors for thirty-five cents a dozen. This paid for our feed, and we even had some leftover to buy something special for our chickens.

It was now 1941. I had just returned home from the movies on Sunday, December 7, and I heard on the radio with my family that the Japanese had bombed Pearl Harbor. I asked my father, "Where is Pearl Harbor?" He told us that it was in Honolulu, Hawaii.

Albert was now eighteen years old, and he received his draft notice to report to duty. He was told to join the Army Air Corps if possible. This way he would be safe and always have a hot meal, a clean bed, and good food to eat. Albert was lucky. He was selected to be in the Army Air Corps. He was also selected to report to mechanic school. Later, after he had attended special training, he was ready to ship out. He was again lucky. He didn't go to Europe but to the Pacific. After General McArthur returned to the Philippines, he was stationed in Luzon, and then later he was shipped to Okinawa to service the aircraft that would strike back at the Japanese. After the war, Albert was sent to Korea, and in 1945, he was stationed at the Wonson Airport in North Korea.

Albert had a lot of buddies who used to come to our house for dinner, but I always liked his friend Jack Craven. He was the only one out of all of Albert's friends to join the United States Marine Corps. He was later assigned to the Fourth Marine Division and fought on many islands, where he was wounded in his left leg. After a stay in the hospital, he returned to his outfit and landed on Iwo Jima and was wounded a second time in the same knee. The second injury was serious enough for him to be shipped home. When he came to visit us, he wore his dress blues, and from then on, I was convinced that I would join the Marines.

In 1941, we had a new baby boy named Joseph who later died. Then again in the same year, there was another boy named James, and soon after him we had another boy named Daniel, and then a year later another boy named Louis. This was the final baby for the Santors.

I became very active in the Boy Scouts, collecting old bottles and rags to earn money so that I could attend camps during the summer. I became very good at camping and cooking and learning how to read a compass. I also learned how to survive in the winter weather—little did I know that this would come in very handy later in life. The only thing I regretted was not being able to attain the rank of Eagle Scout. I was very close to earning all my merit badges, but when I turned fifteen years old, my father said he had sold our house and informed us that we were moving to California. Our oldest brother Albert was already there.

In 1946, my father bought a 1941 Chevrolet sedan for our trip. Boy, this was really something. Picture my father, my mother, Richard, myself, James, Daniel, and Louie, who was just a little baby, all crammed into our 1941 Chevrolet, and we were off to California. This was 1946, and boy, what a trip this was. None of us had ever been out of Buffalo, New York, before. To this day, I don't remember what states we went through, but I do remember Arizona. It was here that we were told that we were going to sleep all day and travel very early in the evening so that we would be crossing the desert at night because it would be cooler. I was told to fill our canvas bag with water to hang it over our radiator to keep it cool, and then we were ready to cross the desert. There we were in California, and looking at the mountains, I had never seen anything like them before. It was the same for the orange, lemon, and grapefruit trees. We had never seen them before. California was so bright with clear blue skies and the weather was very warm for a change.

Upon our arrival in California, we went to our Uncle Mike and Aunt Patty's home. They lived in Glendale, and we were told we would be living with them. Boy, we had a home to live in, and in Glendale, Uncle Mike's house was by the airport, where I used to go and watch all the fighter planes land. They sure were big and beautiful.

CHAPTER 3

OUR NEW LIFE

When we settled into Uncle Mike's home in July of 1946, we started to check out the local schools. We found one close by in Burbank that was not too far from our home. It was called John Buroughs, and we were enrolled there to begin in September. I told my father that I would like to play the trumpet like him, because he played in a band years ago. He said he would help me, and I got to be so good at it that I was given first chair and was asked if I would like to play "The Star-Spangled Banner" at the start of school. I accepted along with my new friend named Ray Anthony, who later in life started his own band. There was also a very timid girl in my class. She later became a very gifted actress; her name was Debbie Reynolds. It seemed that we had many gifted boys and girls who would later in life become well-known actors and actresses. It was at this point that I enrolled for sheet metal and woodshop classes which became very useful later. As the school years went by, I enrolled in orchestra class and took up the French horn. That was something new for me since the catholic schools in Buffalo, New York, did not have shop or orchestra classes.

Uncle Mike's home had become too small for our family, and my father, with the help of my older brother, Albert, bought a much larger home in Burbank. It was a lot closer to our school. Our new home was a lot bigger than Uncle Mike's, because it had three bedrooms where the twins and Elizabeth slept in one bedroom, Albert, Richard, and I shared a second bedroom, and the three little boys shared another room in that was supposed to be the den. Our father and mother slept in the third bedroom. We only had one bathroom, and sometimes it was a problem, since my sister Elaine liked to take her time in there—at least fifteen or twenty minutes at a time. We continued our studies at the same school. I wanted to join the Marines when school was finished but needed my parents' signatures to join since I was only seventeen years old. My father was not too happy when he found out I wanted to join the Marines, but I talked him into signing for me, especially when I told him that the house was too small, and the younger boys would have more room. He finally signed for me, and I was going to be a United States Marine.

CHAPTER 4

JOINING THE MARINES

In February 1948, my father drove me to Los Angeles where the Marine Corps Recruiting Office was located, for me to sign up and take my physical. I was one out of ten that passed (eating all those bananas sure helped to meet the weight requirement) and I was sworn in. They gave me a bus ticket to San Diego, which back then I had no idea where that was. After saying goodbye to the family, I boarded a Greyhound bus and was now on my first adventure.

It took forever to arrive at the San Diego Recruit Depot, and it was almost midnight. I was placed in a room called "the holding section" until there were enough men to form a platoon. Around 12:20 a.m., a large sergeant came into the room and asked if we were hungry. We stated that we were, and he said in a very loud voice, "Good, I'll have some horse cock sandwich brought up." *My god*, I thought, *these Marines eat horse cocks?* And if they do, I want to go home! We found out later that the sandwiches were baloney, so I decided to stay and see what else I would find out.

It wasn't very long before we had enough recruits to form our platoon, and the first item was to receive our military one-eighth haircut. The next thing was to receive our uniforms (that were all too large), and then came the PX supplies and a bucket to store them. We were then shown what would be our new home for the next sixteen weeks and we got our bedding. It was really something to get used to the food and the names they called it, and my favorite was the white

15

cream gravy with hamburger on toasted bread called SOS, or known as shit on a shingle. My next favorite was liver which was called "nigger steak," and the last was French toast, that was called "queer toast." Something we never had at home was Tabasco hot sauce, and so this would be the start of my sixteen weeks of recruit training.

It was very hard to stay awake in the hot classrooms, sitting through the many hours of Marine history and tradition, and learning about the battles they fought during all the years since 1775. It was very interesting and soon I started to feel like a Marine. We were told that in three weeks' time we would be taken by bus to the Camp Mathews Rifle Range. We would be at the range for three weeks and live in tents without hot water or stoves to keep us warm, and to me, this was like camping out with the Boy Scouts. Camp Mathews was a World War II camp where Marines would become accustomed to all the weapons Marines used and would learn how to shoot them. Well, being a city boy, I had never fired a rifle or any other kind of weapon, but I soon learned. After getting my first kick on the recoil and falling back on my ass, I learned not to buck my shots. Now it became fun, and I learned to first start on the small bore, then moved on to the Browning automatic rifle and then the M-1. This was a .30 caliber shell weapon. The small bore was a .22 caliber, and there was quite a difference. We learned to snap in, which was sighting in on a target, squeezing the trigger, and then breathing a sigh of relief. On the third week, we got to qualify with the M-1. If we did good on the rifle range, we would get to sit out in the rain and watch a movie. We also learned that every Marine is a rifleman.

Over the next month, we trained in hand-to-hand combat, close-order drill, which was marching in formation, and how to kill Russians. Now isn't it funny, about killing Russians. Even today we are still talking about killing Russians. The last day of boot camp finally arrived, and it was graduation day. They fed us better than usual, and after dressing in our finest dress blue uniforms, we were off to the parade field and proceeded to graduate. We were given our Eagle, Globe, and Anchor emblems and we were now United States Marines. We were given our pay and we all received a thirty-day furlough. Then we each got on a bus and headed back home.

I remember when we arrived and formed our first platoon, that our goal was to live long enough to kill our drill instructor because he made our lives a living hell. Then on graduation day, when he came into our squad bay and said, "Congratulations on becoming a Marine," it was only at this time that we saw that he was just doing his job. We realized it was his job to see that all of us hated him so that we would survive. He really was a good guy after all.

Thinking back on it, I really enjoyed boot camp. It sort of reminded me of home, with lots of yelling and fighting at the dinner table, and my father threatening to kill us all. He always stated that he should have raised pigs, because when they were grown up, he could kill and eat them. I related this to my drill instructor and why I was so happy all the time, and he said he always had the same thoughts. His name was Sergeant Corbilt, and he was built like a bulldog and had a voice like a foghorn. He turned out to be a great Marine and a nice guy.

We are now ready to leave San Diego Marine Recruit Depot, and after we got paid and packed our gear, we headed home. We would get our orders after returning to base from our thirty-day leave, and we were to report to the Joseph F. Pendleton Marine Base for future combat training. We all said goodbye to all our new friends and hoped to see or serve with them in the future.

CHAPTER 5

HOME FOR THIRTY DAYS

I was now home after sixteen weeks of boot camp, and it felt good to see all my family. The first thing on my agenda was to return to my old school and to see all my old friends. But somehow it wasn't the same because they all seemed like little kids, and it felt that I had nothing in common with them. I did enjoy talking with my old teachers, especially with Ms. French, my music teacher. I remembered how hard it was for me to stay with the beat and in tune when she started to swing her arms in time with the music. She had very large breasts and she always wore tight sweaters. Boy, those were the days. I also visited my shop teachers. They all wished me well and to be careful. I never returned to my old school again.

All my brothers and sisters seemed to be grown-up now. My oldest brother Al had joined the Los Angeles Police Department and was given the walking beat in downtown Hollywood. He said that he liked his new job. He also started insisting that I should have joined the air force and told me all about the good things about air force life. To this day I have never regretted joining the Marine Corps. My brother Richard was bitter because when he joined the Marine Corps, he was discharged after they found out that he cheated on his eye exam. He would remember all the letters on the eye chart until one day they got suspicious and changed the charts. He later joined the army, since they didn't seem to care if you had one good eye or not.

We went to my Aunt Josephine's restaurant to see all the rest of the family, and as usual, they had a big meal for all of us. I got to visit all my cousins. They wanted to know why I chose to join the Marines, since out of all the military members of our family, I was the first Marine. My answer was that I wanted to see and have some new experiences in life. Boy, was I in for a big surprise.

It was really great to eat my mother's home-cooked meals. I'd never realized how much I missed her cooking and how good her spaghetti and meatballs were. She also made home-baked bread and other good Italian foods. My time at home passed very fast and soon it was time to say goodbye to everyone. I told them I would be stationed very close to home and that I would get home whenever I could.

CHAPTER 6

BACK TO CAMP

I returned back to camp and was told that I would be joining B (Baker) Company of the First Battalion, Fifth Marines as a rifleman. It was there that we received our skills as a rifle company. In August of 1948, we were told that the Fifth Marines would be going to Israel on a combat mission, so we were all combat loaded and waiting on the San Diego docks, waiting for final orders from the White House. The president gave orders to stand down, so we returned back to base. In late August, we were told that they were looking for one hundred men to train for a Raiders Group who would be working off a submarine. I jumped at this chance since this is what I was looking for. Once we were grouped together, we started freshwater training. It was at Margarita Lake which was next to the base hospital. This training was to teach us how to capsize our ten-man rubber boat, and then learn how to right it, which was getting the boat back in its original shape. On one of our training days during very warm weather, the water was calm, and when we capsized our boat, I came up from under the water and discovered that I was under the boat. We had been told that there was a pocket of air under the boat and not to panic, but anyhow, I could hear them yelling, "Where is Santor?" I started to wave my arms to let them know I was under the boat. Then the shitheads grabbed my arms and yanked me back into the boat. I felt like I must have swallowed five gallons of water. Afterward when

I gave them a piece of my mind, they said they thought I was drowning and waving my arms in my last efforts. What a day that was.

After that we started our saltwater training at the beach. We were taught how to launch the boat on the surf and how to stay afloat. When we got good at this, we were told to board the submarine and set out to sea and then we would return to the beach. What a laugh that was! After a few attempts, we never made it back dry. We continued this over and over in the daylight hours. When we got good, we were told that in the morning we were going to convoy down to Coronado Amphibious base for submarine training. We were introduced to the boat crew on the submarine *Perch* (SS-313), a WWII-era submarine that had been converted with a large airtight cargo deck behind the conning tower, where we were to store our rubber boats and gear. Our first trip was at night, so around 2330 hours we climbed aboard and got our bunk locations. The bunks were eight high, so I grabbed a top bunk. Next, we were told to report to the ship's galley for coffee and food if we were hungry, which were silly questions to ask Marines. The sub skipper informed us that we would be spending our first experience as Marines with the US Navy, which was underwater for over ten days without surfacing. As if we had a say in this. It was very peaceful under the water; in fact it was so quiet that we could hear fish scraping along the side of the submarine. The food was great, and we had lots of time to relax, watch movies, read books, or just sleep. After two days of this, we asked the skipper if we could stand watch along with the crew. He said that we could stand in for periscope or helms watch. I jumped at this, selecting the periscope watch. The skipper said that if I saw anything unusual that I was to sound the alarm. Everything went great for the first few minutes, until I decided to turn around 180 degrees, when I noticed that there was this large object following us at the same speed we were going. I hit the horn button and the skipper came running to find out the problem. I explained to him that there was this large object following our sub and at the same speed. He shook his head and said a few choice words, then said that the object following us was our snorkel tube. The snorkel tube is a smokestack that allows the sub to use its engines underwater to recharge the ship's batteries. That was the last time I volunteered on the sub.

After our ten days of being submerged, we were told that we would be making our first nighttime landing. This was great news, since we could not wait to exit off the sub. Our naval intelligence told us that the surf was calm, not over twelve inches high, and the water was at its normal temperature for January. We got our gear, went topside to enter our boats, shoved off the sub, and the next thing I noticed, the sub was gone, and we were alone two miles off the beach. It was such a black night, with no moon and the stars were completely hidden by clouds. When we got our bearings, we started to move with the flow of the tide. We started ashore and we could hear the surf pounding about a mile offshore; so much for twelve-inch waves. When we got to the surf line, we started to head in, and oh, boy, what a ride. Our bowman dropped the bow, and we shot through the air like a sling shot. Well, so much for getting in dry. We got trucked back to our base and got some shut-eye. Tomorrow would be another exciting day.

This training went on until January. Then we boarded the sub, stowed our gear, and waited for orders. It came over the intercom that we would be joining a group of other ships for training. Everything seemed normal while we were watching a movie. I noticed the ship's porter entering our compartment and suddenly there was a terrible crash. The porter followed his training and quickly closed and secured our watertight door. The sub rocked back and forth and started to sink as we hung on to our bunk rails and the movie camera until it was finally safe to let go. We stopped sinking and sat at the bottom and were told to check for damage or water seepage and found that there was none. We decided to watch the end of the movie. We stayed submerged for three to five hours, but who was watching the time? We were told if things got bad, we were to reverse our hatch and flood the compartment, so we could open the outer hatch, release the line, and prepare to don our Momsen air lungs. Once we left the sub, we were told that there was a knot every ten feet, and to stop, breathe in for ten counts, and continue on until we came to next knot and to follow this until we reached the surface. Just when we were preparing to reverse the hatch, the skipper came on and informed us we were going to try and surface. When we finally reached the surface, it was like daylight. I had never seen so many search lights and it looked like the whole fleet was there. I did notice that when I went through the forward hatch there was a huge propeller on the forward deck, and I thought, *Boy, I wonder how many pennies that would make.* We returned to base and were told not to speak to any reporters. Three weeks later, our group was disbanded, and we found out that our sub damage was about $1.5 million.

CHAPTER 7

KOREA

In late September, we were informed to start packing our gear, because we were going to Tsingtao, China, to reinforce the Sixth Marines there. It seems that General Chiang Kai-shek was being driven out by the Chinese Communist Party and needed our help. Well, here we go again, all loaded with our combat equipment, off to San Diego waiting to board our ship, and when the word came down, President Truman said to stand down, and we had to return to base. It seems that General Chang Kai-shek was pushed back to Formosa, leaving all the American combat equipment, trucks, jeeps, ammo, 105 mm and 155 mm howitzers, and small arms behind. Those Marines were transported back to stateside and then back to Camp Pendleton, and later transferred back east to form the Sixth Marines.

We are now entering January 1950, and I figured that I would never leave California during my enlistment term, but just weeks later, I received the word that I was being transferred to Bangor. *Great*, I thought, *I was going to Bangor, Maine*. Wrong, I'm going to Bangor, Washington, but where the hell is Bangor, Washington? It's not even on the map. It was a Navy Ammunition Depot in Washington state, close to Bremerton on the Puget Sound, population 125 including the livestock. The ammo depot was where all the US Navy ships went to reload their ammunition supply before heading out to sea. After a train ride from California and a ferry ride across Puget Sound, I finally arrived in Bangor. The base had sixty enlisted Marines, two officers, and one base commander. Our job was to stand watch at the front gate, patrol the docks and ammo dumps, and to secure the base grounds. My job was jeep patrol for four hours on and eight hours off, seven days a week. Our quarters had its own cook, and there was a post exchange for supplies, a movie theater, bowling lanes, and a brig.

One day on patrol, I noticed two young boys running through the trees on the base. I stopped my jeep and gave chase, and when I caught up with them, I was confronted by a very good-looking young lady. She informed me that the two young boys were her brothers and that they were the camp commander's children. I apologized and turned them loose. I informed them not to run away but to stop and talk with the Marine security guard on duty. We became very good friends after this. In fact, all four of us would go to the movies on the base whenever we got the chance. All the Marines on the base would tease me for seeing her, and I became very fond of her. Sometime later I was told that she had been in an auto accident, was thrown through the windshield, and would never be the same. It took me some time to get over this. Her father later became head of the FBI. Her name was Chloe Kelly.

I really liked being stationed in Bangor. I had never seen so many wild fruit trees in my life! I would stop and fill my cover with cherries or whatever fruit was ripe to pick, then continue with my patrol and eat cherries. Boy, what a life.

Little did I know that soon my perfect life in the Marines was going to end. It was on June 25, 1950, that the announcement came over the radio that the North Korean communist troops had crossed the Thirty-Eighth parallel and invaded South Korea. We talked about it and decided that President Truman would not call their bluff into fighting this war. We were wrong, and we were given the word that we were going to get on board trains and travel to Camp Pendleton to form the First Marine Division. At this time the Marine Corps only had eighty thousand regular active-duty Marines. They had to call on all their guard units and also make up the difference by calling the Marine Corps Reserve in order to form a division of twenty-six thousand men. We were told that we were going to form

Charlie Company, First Battalion, First Marines, and that our regimental commander was going to be Chesty Puller. What a privilege to have Chesty Puller as our commander because he was awarded five navy crosses and many other awards. He was the most decorated Marine in the Marine Corps. When Charlie Company was formed, they were looking for volunteers to become machine gunners. Well, I didn't like being a rifleman, so I volunteered to be a gunner. I was assigned as seventh ammo carrier. That meant I had to carry two cans of ammo for the gun. Great, so if I'm the last ammo carrier, that means I would be in the rear. This wasn't the case, but I will talk about this later. We were stationed at tent camp two, which was way back on the outskirts of the camp. We were really training very hard, running drills, and firing live ammo with the machinegun.

It was in early July 1950, and there we were, fully equipped with weapons, gear, and fully staffed companies, formed up to deploy to Korea. It came to the week for deployment, and I remember I was lying on my bunk when one of my friends came into the hut said, "Hey, Santor, there are a bunch of Santors here to see you." I jumped up, ran outside, and there they were, my parents, my sister, and a few of my uncles and aunts. They came to see me off. We talked, hugged, and kissed goodbye and then they left. My buddies were very jealous of me. The next few days, we started to board the ships and kept waiting for the word from President Truman to stand down, but it never came. We traveled to San Diego to board ship and began to sail out of San Diego harbor. Boy, I have never seen so much ocean as we were heading to Kobe, Japan. It took ten long days to travel. Life on board a ship is very boring because there is nothing to do. We would read, sleep, eat, go to class, and fire our weapons. A few days after landing in Kobe, Japan, there came a warning of a typhoon heading for Kobe. It was too late to head out to the open sea, so they decided to ride it out tied to the docks. They told all Marines to go below, lock your quarters, and ride out the storm. Boy, talk about a cork in the below deck quarters; it was so hot and miserable, and we were being tossed around like a pinball. I tried to sleep and didn't want to stay in my bunk, but it turns out we had to ride it out to the end. Typhoon Finley was finally over, and we were let out of the ship, but what a mess! Small ships were sitting on land, with broken piers everywhere. Our ship lines were broken like someone cut them. After this little ride, we were given liberty, but we were told we could not eat any Japanese food or fruit. My buddies and I stopped at a small bar and had some beers for fifteen cents a quart, and they served us some crunchies. They were very good until we asked what they were, and oh my, they were fried grasshoppers. No, thank you, we said and left to return to the ship.

We were finally fully loaded with ammo and materials for our landing in Korea. Again, we boarded our ship and set sail for Korea. Our job was to be on the first wave, to land at Blue Beach, to cut off the North Koreans, and then we were to return to Incheon and then return home to the states. Wrong again, Charlie Company would be on the first wave to land at Blue Beach on September 15, 1950. Our job was to storm the sea wall and get in on the incoming thirty-five-foot tide. We were told to get a good night's rest and then prepare to board our landing crafts the next day. On the morning of September 17, the navy cut loose with salvos of rockets and the ship's heavy guns for over six hours. Then our Navy and Marine Air Groups hit them with rockets, machine-gun fire, and five-hundred-pound bombs. We loaded into our Higgins Boats to land at our designated beach. The other companies got lost in the rain or smoke and landed on the wrong beaches. We scaled the seawall and headed inland, and since we had very little resistance, we settled down for the night to try and get dry and warm.

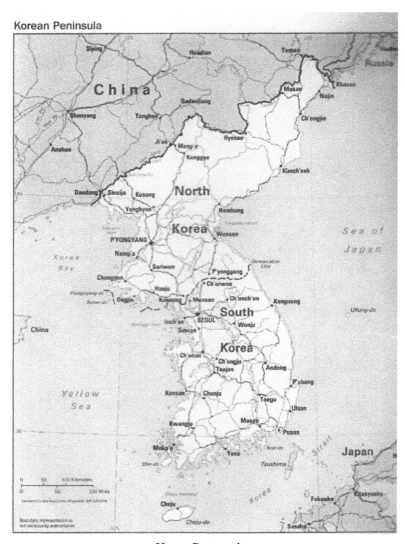

Korea Peninsula.

Red Beach, Green Beach, and Blue Beach area of operations.

Department of Defense Photo (USMC) A5190

Marines go over the seawall forming the sharp edge of Red Beach. The Marine on the ladder has been identified as 1stLt Baldomero Lopez. Moments later he would give his life and earn a posthumous Medal of Honor.

Moving through a rice paddy.

CHAPTER 8

HILL 85

Our trip through Japan on the way to Korea was very monotonous. Our ship was an old WWII APA, and it was in pretty good shape, very clean, and it seemed that the whole First Regiment was aboard our ship. The crew and food were pretty good, considering the number of Marines they had to feed. Our days aboard were occupied with getting to know our machine guns and firing them off the fantail.

One day, my friend George Kinnick, whom I had known from boot camp, and I decided to start a scuttlebutt rumor. Three days later, it returned to our company and made it down to our machine-gun squad, and when we heard it, it was turned around so much that we believed it.

One thing that the crew had told us was to tie a line through your belt loop before you throw your trousers overboard to wash them and you won't lose them. Of course. this handy hint came a little too late because some Marines had already lost their clothes.

When we got to Kobe, Japan, we volunteered to help the ship's crew load the ship with ammunition and supplies. This made our days go faster.

Several days after the typhoon had subsided, we completed the reloading and then set sail to Korea, although we were not told our destination until we were at sea. We were told that we would land at Incheon and try to cut the North Koreans off.

The next day we assumed a tactical formation and began to move eastward toward Seoul. Our opposition was light, and we came upon some small arms fire. Our platoon squad leader put us and our gun into direct fire and left us. After the fight, I told our squad leader that I was going to give that bastard a piece of my mind. He told me not to do that, and I answered, "What the hell is he going to do to me? I am the seventh ammo carrier, no one is lower than me." Then I told that shithead, "Next time you do that to us, I am going to kill you." Then guess what, that shithead made me the gunner. After this happened, we moved fairly rapidly while maintaining security against a counterattack. The weather during the day was very hot and humid, and since everyone was carrying a full pack, weapons, and ammunition, some of the Marines began to fall out from the heat. Among the heaviest loads they were carrying were the mortars and flamethrowers. We had to climb over numerous hills, and more and more men were passing out. We had a company jeep, and luckily, they were allowed to ride in it. Before we got to Kimpo Airfield, we came upon a beautiful sight. It seemed that the whole valley was covered with these beautiful red flowers, but when we got closer, we saw that they were not flowers but little red peppers. I picked one and took a small bite, and oh my god, it felt like someone stuck a knife in my stomach! Man, they were so hot, I almost died. After this, we continued on to Kimpo Airfield, and when we passed it, we approached Hill 80. Our machine squad came upon a burst of automatic fire from a schoolhouse. I was lying on my stomach when all hell broke out. It felt like someone punched me in my back and then I felt hot liquid running down my back. I asked George to take a look, and he started to laugh. "What the hell is so funny?" I said, and when he stopped laughing, he said, "Remember that can of peaches you had? Well, forget it, it has a big hole in it." I was really mad then and put our gun into action to fire directly at the source of fire. We called our rocket man forward and instructed him to fire on a small opening that was about twelve by twelve inches and told him to fire. To our amazement, he sent the shell right through the opening and knocked out the shooter. We had a very hard time with him later, seeing this put a feather in his cap. Much later, Able Company assumed our foxholes, and they proceeded to charge the schoolhouse and planted an American flag on its roof. This gave us a laugh, seeing that we had knocked it out. However, after we had knocked out the schoolhouse, a local South Korean approached us carrying a little girl in his arms and she was dead. Somehow, she had been in a tunnel with her grandfather and looked out to see what was happening. One of the Marine riflemen thought that she was a North Korean soldier and shot her. I will never forget the look on her grandfather's face. We never found out who fired that shot. It has been over seventy-two years that this memory of that little girl lying in her grandfather's arms still haunt me to this day.

One thing that has bothered me, even to this date. It was after this that I needed some sort of fire protection since I only had a .45 caliber pistol and that was all. I decided to cut about thirty to forty rounds off my gun ammo belt and started to carry my machine gun on my hip. It was then and there that I picked up my nick name "Shoot Them From the Hip Sammy." Ever since then, whenever I get a phone call from any of my buddies, they say "Hey, is this Shoot Them From the Hip Sammy?" For the attack on Hill 85, Lieutenant Commisky was to attack with his third platoon, and Lieutenant Guild was to attack with our gun section. I set the gun up to cover fire. When Lieutenant Guild started up the hill, he was shot in the upper chest and stomach and fell. He died later that night. Lieutenant Commisky continued on up the hill and knocked out two machine gun positions and secured the hill. After this, Lieutenant Commisky was presented with the Congressional Medal of Honor, the first Marine to receive this award in Korea. Lieutenant Commisky was also a WWII veteran and fought on Iwo Jima as an enlisted man. As I was giving the second platoon cover, Reed, a rifleman, yelled to me, "Santor, move over the hill. There is a T-34 tank preparing to shoot at you." And sure enough, the minute that I moved over the hill, the tank shot at me and missed me. Reed had just saved my life.

Later after we moved out, I went by the tank, which was destroyed by our Marine planes, looked inside, and saw that the dead tank crew were all Russian soldiers. Later we found out that all the tank crews were Russian soldiers.

CHAPTER 9

CITY OF SEOUL

Charlie Company was now known as Loping Charlie Company, and the reason was that we never walked to get where we were going, we always ran.

After Hill 85, we saddled up to move out so we would be leaving Yeongdeungpo and then crossing the Han River into the town of Seoul. After we crossed the Han River in "ducks," we settled into a small village where all the townspeople were cheering and waving flags. The order came down to get comfortable and dig in for the night. Well, there was no space to dig our gun pit because we were in a heavy population. We asked an older Korean woman if we could stay inside her house, and she said yes, so we dug our gun pit in her kitchen and ended up having a perfect view of downtown Seoul. It was a very peaceful night, and when we woke up in the morning, we found that the Korean mamasan had covered all of us with blankets. We were so sorry that we dug up her kitchen, and after looking around her house, there was not one item of food that we could see. The squad dug into their backpacks and removed all our C rations and gave them to the lady. She was so happy she started to cry.

The word came down that loping Charlie Company would lead the attack at the train depot and the second platoon would be in the lead. The minute we turned the corner, all hell broke loose because there were snipers in every building that was over two stories high, and it was very hard to spot them with the smokeless powder that they used.

We noticed that there was a flamethrower tank close by, and we asked for it to come to our rescue and to put its muzzle into all windows and let it rip. Problem was solved, no more snipers. The closer we got to the train station, the heavier the action got. We were really catching hell when we were told to cross the street and get into the station. I started to cross the street, and as I was running, I saw Crews laying in the street. I asked him where he was hit, and he looked at me and said one of the snipers shot him in the ass as he was running for cover. I said, "Do you need some help?" He started to yell at me and said, "Get your ass in the station!" I said okay and started for the door, and as I looked down, I noticed something went between my legs. At that moment, it felt just as if someone gave me a push and I was safe inside the building before "it" hit the wall and exploded. I found out later that it was a Russian anti-tank rifle that was shooting at me. Thank you, God. Later a projectile from the battleship *Missouri* sent out a sixteen-inch shell in front of the station. It made a gigantic hole that you would not believe. Along came one of our tanks. It struck a North Korean land mine that was right in front of our crater. I watched as the tank rose a foot off the ground from the explosion. The crew was okay, but they ended up losing a track. I noticed that I was bleeding bad, but I was so pumped up on adrenaline that I continued on.

We continued chasing those North Koreans and drove them over the thirty-eighth parallel, and as the firefights died down, we were able to take a break from the heat and fire in the buildings. We found some shelter and settled in for the evening. When we got settled, I noticed that the strap on my helmet had a bullet hole dead center (oh my god!). A few inches and it would've hit me in the throat. Again, I checked my gun and noticed that there was a bullet hole in one of the tripod leg. Thank you, God, and or my guardian angel for watching over me.

The very next day, they told me to man the gun at our outpost, which was in front on Charlie's second platoon line. George and I were sitting there when we heard someone coming. And well, look who was here. It was Lieutenant Commisky with two containers of beer. "Lieutenant, where did you find the beer?" He said that when we went through Yeongdeungpo, there was a beer factory, and he confiscated a barrel of beer for Charlie Company. Boy, that sure did hit the spot!

Photo by Frank Noel, Associated Pr

Front-line Marines found that stripping a prisoner bare took all the fight out
him and also eliminated the possibility of hidden weapons. Rear-echelon auth
ities found the practice distasteful and ordered the Marines to desist.

Overlooking Seoul.

Outskirts of Seoul.

This page and the next, street fighting in Seoul as captured by Life magazine photographer David Douglas Duncan.

Street fighting in Seoul as captured by *Life* magazine
photographer David Douglas Duncan.

Seoul train station.

The tank was moving past the crater when it hit a mine and
lifted about six inches off the deck, blowing a track.

We dove into the sixteen-inch crater to take
cover after the tank hit the mine.

CHAPTER 10

BACK TO INCHEON

We were relieved by the army and returned back to Incheon, and I checked into sick bay and had them look at my arm. They removed some shrapnel and gave me a shot of penicillin, then dressed my wound and sent me back to my company.

We were told that we were there because we had to replace our wounded and dead to bring our company back to strength. The scuttlebutt was that after we were up to full strength that we were going home. Wrong, we were going to board ships again to move north. We were told to enjoy our two or three days there and to have a good time. Great, this was a good time to check out the town. While I was in the city, I saw a civilian selling fresh eggs and so I asked how much they were. When he told me, I said I didn't have any money, and he asked what did I have to trade? I remembered that a day before they had handed out some long johns, but they didn't have my size. The egg man asked for some clothing, and all I had was what I was wearing, but wait, I knew that George had a pair. I told the Korean that I'd be right back, and I ran back to our encampment, grabbed George's long johns, and returned to town. The Korean's eyes got really wide, and he gave me three dozen eggs for them. I rushed back to my crew and said, "Look what I've got, who wants to cook them?" George volunteered and he cooked all the eggs. Later when we were finished eating, George asked me where I got the money for the eggs, and the whole gun crew perked up and asked me, "Where did you get the money?" Well, I said I didn't have any money, so I traded a pair of long johns for them, and George said, "You didn't have a pair 'cause they didn't have your size?" I told him, "Well, George, I can't lie to you, I traded your long johns for the eggs," and George chased me all over our camp, but I was a faster runner than him.

A few days later, Charlie Company and a company from the amphibian battalion loaded aboard an LST (Landing Ship Tank), an ocean-going military ship for moving troops and equipment. We sailed south around the southern tip of the Incheon peninsula, and then we headed back north toward Wonson. For over a week, we continued to sail north during the day, and toward evening, we would reverse our course and head south. This was dubbed "Operation Yo-Yo." Rumors flew when we were heading south, that the Korean War was over and shortly would be heading home. Wrong again, because in reality we were merely biding time while the navy minesweeper was clearing a path through an estimated ten thousand mines that the North Koreans had set in and around Wonsan Harbor.

An LST is not designed for a lot of people and on this one was our company of over two hundred officers and enlisted Marines. The crews of some thirteen landing crafts were also on board, so it was really crowded. For sleeping quarters, they had a few officers with individual rooms, and then the captain's quarters, and he was a navy lieutenant. They also had a few chiefs' quarters, but they were full of the ship's chiefs. We had two staff NCOs on board who were master sergeants. They had no place to sleep except on a very hard deck like the rest of us because there were simply no quarters for them. The captain finally agreed to let them sleep in the officers' quarters, and they could also eat meals in the officers' country.

For the rest of us, we slept below in the tank deck. It was not too bad except when we hit rough water. The spot I had was in the center of the ship, and it felt like it was bending in the middle, and it kept me awake all night. I was told later that the ship was designed that way because of the heavy load of the tractors or tanks. Life was not too bad, just the food was bad. Again, while going back and forth, life was pretty boring. We slept or played cards, and we would run around the upper deck when the weather was nice. Life got bad when we ran into a typhoon again, but LSTs are not designed for comfort. Up and down, up and down, and everyone was seasick, even the crew, but not me, I loved it.

We finally arrived in Wonson Harbor one evening and anchored until morning. Shortly after breakfast, we loaded aboard the amphibian tractors and prepared to depart in the LSTs, but this rapidly developed into more of a problem than anticipated. When the front ramp on the LST was lowered, it stuck in a position some seventeen degrees above the horizontal, and it would not lower anymore. Then a powerful navy chief wielding a sixteen-pound sledgehammer slammed the chains on both sides of the stuck ramp with all his force but without success. The ramp should have come to rest in a position seventeen degrees below the horizontal before discharging troops, so you can see the reason for the chief's concern.

The captain of the LST suggested that the weight of the first amphibian tractor might break the ramp loose so that we could make a normal departure. The captain knew that we had a schedule to keep, and we had to get ashore immediately so that we could start unloading the amphibian tractors.

The command group would take the first tractor off the ramp, and the tractor operator drove it up and off the slanted ramp into the bay. Now that was an experience. Instead of entering the water in approximately level attitude as normal, the raised ramp caused them to go nose first at a very steep angle. It was over in just a minute, and after playing submarine, it gradually came to the surface while the engine was sputtering, and everyone was breathing a huge sigh of relief. The remaining twelve amphibian tractors with Charlie Company aboard climbed up the defective ramp and entered the water at that steep angle and with a great splash. We all made it, but almost half of them had their engines drowned out due to the long time they were underwater, and they had to be towed ashore.

Department of Defense Photo (USMC) A4313

Finally off the ships, the First Marine Division, which ended its interminable "Operation Yo-Yo" on October 26, chugs ashore by Navy LCVP toward Wonsan, North Korea.

Department of Defense Photo (USN) 421366

In the anticlimactic landing of the First Marine Division at Wonsan, troops dismount from a column of LVT-3Cs and their escorting LVTA-5 armored amphibians along the Wonsan airfield. A chill wind blows in from the looming Taebaek Mountains.

CHAPTER 11

WONSAN

After arriving ashore in Wonsan, we were placed aboard several cars on a local train and headed south toward the town of Kojo. Our ability to defend ourselves while traveling on open flat rail was severely limited and caused a great deal of concern. This was because we were told before we left Wonsan that there were many North Korean troops in the area, and they were working their way north to rejoin their units. The pucker factor was especially raised when we went into an unlit tunnel. I had visions of enemy troops blasting both ends of the tunnel and sealing us inside, and the thought did not appeal to me. It was probably close to five or ten minutes of darkness and fear before we left the tunnel and the light of day looked very good to us.

When we arrived in Kojo, we found that the job we were sent to do had disappeared. Colonel Hawkin's order had been that our battalion was to secure and guard a supply depot that the ROK Army had abandoned in the face of large number of North Korean troops, who were working their way north to rejoin friendly troops after being defeated by the First Marine Brigade in an operation to the south of us. Colonel Hawkins saw that the supply dump was gone, and he went by the book, which says when a commander finds himself without a mission, he derives one, based on the situation he faces. The information available to Colonel Hawkins was that large numbers of disorganized enemy stragglers were in the area, working their way northward. He decided to place units of the battalion in blocking positions to prevent those forces from rejoining other enemy units, a logical mission if the available intelligence was correct.

Able Company was to provide security to the battalion headquarters which was spread out on the top of a hill overlooking the bay of Kojo. Baker Company was given a blocking position on three small hills to the south of Able's position. Charlie Company was placed on an east-west line to the west of the battalion headquarters. In view of the report of only light, disorganized enemy resistance, both Baker and Charlie companies where thinly spread out in blocking positions. For Charlie Company that meant that we had about a 2,200-yard front, which gave us an average of approximately forty yards between two-man foxholes. That was with all three platoons on the line and nothing in support. Needless to say, in case of any kind of an organized attack by a sizeable force, we would be in trouble. Our easternmost platoon was the third platoon that was led by Lieutenant Comiskey, and they were separated from the Able Company position by about 250 yards. Tied into the third platoon was Lieutenant Craven's platoon, with Lieutenant Carlon's second platoon on the company's west flank. Although we were spread quite thinly, the three platoons were tied in with one another. All available information had indicated that no organized resistance would be encountered, and if there was any, Charlie Company was to hold the assigned position of the ridge in such a manner as to prevent any stragglers or small groups of North Koreans from moving northward to rejoin their units. The employment of three platoons of Charlie Company on the line was necessary due to the length of the ridge that we were required to occupy.

We were dug in on the forward slope of the ridge facing south. Positions were constructed to provide for defense from the rear, in the event enemy elements approached our position from that direction, and a squad from each platoon was in position to provide security in that area. The first indication of enemy activity from the south was the firing of green flares and blowing whistles shortly after dark, about 8:00 p.m. At about the same time, grenades, small arms, machine gun fire, and whistles could be heard from the south in the vicinity of Baker Company's position. All hands were alerted, as we anticipated some enemy contact, and we were not disappointed for long. A few minutes after the firing of green flares started, the North Koreans attacked Lieutenant Carlon's second platoon, initially using grenades. We were forewarned for five to ten minutes by the flares with all hands making every effort to observe any enemy activity. It speaks well of the North Koreans that they were able to creep unobserved and unheard to within easy grenade range of our positions before we could detect them, particularly considering the fact we were expecting enemy activity from that direction.

The attack extended along most of Lieutenant Carlon's platoon and was strongest at the position approximating his east boundary with Lieutenant Craven's first platoon. His right boundary was the west flank of Charlie Company. This was on the western end of the ridge where our positions were located.

I remember looking out in front of my gun, probably within about twelve to eighteen inches, and a North Korean popped up and looked at me, and that is when I shot him. All hell broke loose and grenades were popping all over my position. As I was firing, I remember one grenade started to throw sparks and then it went off, blowing my gun clear out of my fox hole and knocking me back, wounding me in the arm and face. Before I knew it, two more went off, and I looked for my gun, but it was blown clear out and down the hill. I climbed out of my hole and went to the top of the hill, and Sergeant Salesberry told me to follow him down the hill. We started to walk west toward the ocean, and it was just about daybreak when a corsair flew by and waved his wings at us. Shortly thereafter, a truck came and picked us up and transported us back to our lines. I was evacuated off the beach and transported to the hospital ship, *Constellation*.

While in the hospital, I tried to go back and think about what took place twenty-four hours ago, and I could remember when we first got to Kojo. We were on a hill and could see in the distance that around two hundred to three hundred men with black coats on were marching, and this was reported to Colonel Hawkins but he did nothing. That was his first mistake, and his second was placing his companies in a dangerous position, spacing his men too far between foxholes. The third mistake he made was not giving the men time to relax and recover from their long trip on the train. Most of the men in Baker Company died in their sleeping bags due to the long day and from exhaustion. Chesty Puller did the right thing by firing his fat ass and kicking him out of Kojo. I remember firing my gun at point-blank range and figured I killed around ninety or so of those bastards. We lost a handful of good Marines that night and I will never forget them.

While on the hospital ship, they (the doctors) tried to remove all the shrapnel in my face, and they removed all but two, one below my left eye, and the other next to my nose. It was decided to leave these two fragments alone because one was below my left eye muscle, and if they tried to cut it out, I would likely lose the muscle that controls the left eye. The other one was under my right eye. After a day or two, I started to gain my sight back, and I was told that I could return to my company as soon as I could see again.

This was not my main concern because I was told that George was missing after the firefight and that he was considered lost in action. But I knew George could take care of himself and that he would make it back to our lines.

When I was finally discharged from the hospital ship, I checked in at the battalion headquarters, receiving a rifle (my pistol disappeared on the ship after I was checked in), and returned to our company; there was George. I sure was happy to see him again, and I asked him what happened. He said that it was so confusing with so many grenades going off and the shooting all around him, that he was ordered to get to the top of the hill, but then he took a wrong turn and ended up behind the enemy lines. He said he waited until daybreak, and then a North Korean soldier looked him in the eye, turned around, and left, leaving him free to escape and return to our company. "George," I said, "you sure are one lucky Marine! You caused me to lose some sleep worrying about you, but I am so glad that you're all right."

This is a good time to tell the story of Anya Nord. On our way to the north, right before Thanksgiving, I received a package in the mail from my brother Richard. We camped that night between Wonsan and Chinghung-ni. I had assembled our machine gun squad together to open my package that contained some cookies, salami, candy, and a women's model and fashion magazine. After we all took a turn to look through the magazine, George suggested that we choose one of the models to be our pinup girl. After we selected one, it was decided that I would be the one to write to her and explain how we had all chosen her as our favorite model from the magazine. I included my name and the names of our squad members and mailed the letter to the magazine and waited. Around two or three weeks went by, and to our amazement, I received a letter from Anya. She said that my letter was forwarded to her from the editor of the magazine, with a note telling her to contact the Marines. She said that she was a New York part-time model, twenty-four years old, single, and going to college. She was delighted that our machine-gun squad had picked her. We wrote back and forth and really got to know her. She asked if she and her friend could send anything, and our reply was yes, some reading material, pencils, and anything else that they would like to send.

At this time, we were very busy, and mail could not go out or come in due to being surrounded by the Chinese. We didn't receive her mail or packages until we were in Mason, South Korea. Our squad was very happy to get her letters, and boy, the packages were good. I informed her that we lost a few of our members up north and told her how getting mail from her and her friends lifted our spirits when times get rough and that the letters and goodies were really enjoyed by the whole crew. We continued our letters until late April of 1951. I returned to the States and wrote to her that I was home and asked if she would continue writing to the boys. I wrote and told her that George would continue the correspondence with her, and if she wanted to include me in her letters that would be fine. I received a few more letters and then they stopped. I always thought about her, and how we looked forward to her letters and not the war. I aways thought about her and wondered if she continued her schooling or she got married or what happened, but I never found out.

My greatest bitch was that all our mail and packages that were mailed to us never made it. Somewhere down the line, some mail orderly would sniff the package to smell meat or other items that would smell, and they would shake the package to hear a gurgle of liquid. Out of seventeen packages that were sent to me I only received two. This was after my dad placed the sausage and anything that gave a meat odor, he would pack them into a large Quaker Oats canister, place the oats around the items, and this stopped the mail orderlies from sniffing the food. This worked very well! When I returned home and sent my boys liquor and other items, I would fill the bottles up to the brim, tape it very good, insert in the oat container, fill the container with the oats, seal it, and then mail the package. They received every package containing salami, pepperoni, and other items that was food or liquid. This just shows that good old Italian ingenuity never fails.

Gen Oliver P. Smith Collection, Marine Corps Research Center

Men of the 1st Marines sweep through the village of Kojo following the sudden, violent, and well-coordinated North Korean night attacks of 27 October on the 1st Battalion's positions.

CHAPTER 12

CHUNGHUNG-NI

When Charlie Company was ordered to move out up to Chunghung-Ni, I was still recuperating from the wounds. My arm still hurt, and my face was all puffy from the hand grenade that got me in the face. A few days later, we loaded into trucks to form a convoy of six-by-six trucks and started north to join the rest of the battalion at Chunghung-Ni, north of Hamhung. We spent one night near the town of Chunghung-Ni, and an incident took place which illustrates how important it is to keep one's wits in a tactical situation. It also demonstrated how demanding a noncommissioned officer can be, especially when an enemy attack was likely, and how critically important it is to protect a company from thoughtlessness by one of its members.

We were in an area where an enemy attack was likely, and I was dozing off in my sleeping bag at about midnight when a shot rang out. By this time, I was always sleeping very lightly, and I was immediately awake and asked where the shot came from. It seems that our sentries were about thirty yards away, and someone ran over to see what the matter was. We asked the sentry if he fired the shot, and he said, "No, that son of a bitch did, and look at my foot." You could see where the bullet had slammed into the ground next to his foot, and again, we asked the sentry if he fired the shot. He indicated that he had fired it, and he said, "I thought I saw something move." This lack of judgment and sheer stupidity not only endangered a fellow sentry, but it also alerted enemy troops in the area of our presence. It was more than Gunny Krager could take, and he hauled off and hit the sentry hard! The rest of the night was quiet, and the next morning, we climbed aboard our six-by-six trucks and headed north.

We were told to check out the foothills in the area to see if the information was correct. The battalion was told that they got the word that there were South Korean prisoners in that section. We continued to an area by the foothills and saw an orchard full of Korean pear trees. The skipper said to help our self, and boy, did we pig out on them. Our skipper ordered the second platoon squad to check out a cave that we came upon. We set up our gun at the entrance, while a squad of riflemen entered the cave. We heard shots fired, then it was quiet. About five minutes later, a rifleman came running out yelling for the skipper. When the skipper came out of the cave, he called for our corpsmen to join him. Now our machine gun squad was wondering what the hell was going on. It seemed like hours later that they came out. There were over one hundred South Korean young girls that were captured by the North Koreans in early June, and they were from fourteen to thirty-five years old, many of them were in some state of malnutrition. We escorted them back to battalion and that was the last time we saw or heard what happened to them.

The weather was turning very cold, and the clouds and the snow conditions were blinding, The mortar platoons were all out of 60 mm shells and radioed back to Japan that they needed "Tootsie Rolls," and they needed them bad. The supply clerk thought that this was strange, and then a second frantic call came, and he was told to ship all the "Tootsie Rolls" he could find. Either he did not know or did not have his code book that told him that Tootsie Rolls was the code name for 60 mm mortar shells. Well, the weather cleared up and the Tootsie Rolls (the candy) were air dropped to the Marines. Thank God, because not only did this give the Marines a shot in the arm, it also gave them what they needed, which was the sugar for energy, and oh yes, you could follow the Marines by following the wrappers.

We drove through Hungnam and Hamhung, and on through Sudong to Chunghung-Ni, south of the Funchilin Pass. It started to get really cold now, and we still had no warm clothing. We started to dig in where an army artillery battalion had obviously abandoned their positions, leaving neat piles of 155 mm artillery. All around the valley were more shells; more on this story later.

We spent several days digging in and patrolling in all directions. Rumor had it that the Chinese had entered the war, and we were trying to take one or more Chinese prisoners if we encountered them. At this time elements of the Fifth and Seventh Marines and the second and third battalions of the First Marines were heavily engaged to the north of us. As the situation confronting the Eighth Army to the west of us was deteriorating, we were told to wait for further orders. At their positions in Garu-Ri and Yudam-Ni, the First Marine Division were commanded by General Oliver P. Smith, who disregarded orders from the Tenth Corps Commander to continue the advance north of Yudam-Ni. He ordered units at Koto-Ri, Hagaru-Ni, and Yudam-Ni to consolidate their positions and await further orders. While we had been heavily engaged down south in Kojo, they had been advancing into the Chosin Reservoir area, and when we were brought up to Chunghung-Ni, we were in an excellent position to assist the remainder of the division attack over the Funchilin Pass, in the event we were ordered to return south to Hungnam.

Chunghung-Ni was a small village north of Sudong located in a valley. I recall a pretty stream there that flowed freely when the weather warmed up enough for the snow to melt. A couple of times in the early morning quiet, I was able to walk along the stream, and I had the feeling that if it wasn't so cold (down to negative thirty degrees Fahrenheit) and if we were not in a combat situation, it would have been a beautiful little valley. The army had been there before us and had left seven or eight neat stacks of 155 mm ammunition, each alongside a flat spot where a 155 mm howitzer had been parked. It turned out that the unit that had been there had left in a hurry and had abandoned its ammunition. My battalion had assigned each rifle company a portion of the perimeter, and we dug in, placing our outposts in positions to detect any enemy movements into our area. There was extensive patrolling in all directions due to the deteriorating tactical situation to the north that made it very likely that an enemy attack could come from any direction. Charlie Company's position was on the southern portion of the camp and astride the main road which went south to Hungnam, north to Koto-Ri, Hagaru, and Udam-Ni.

When we first arrived in Chunghung-Ni, we had noticed a small army outfit that was about platoon size on the west side of the valley where the town was located. As the tactual situation worsened, we could observe some frantic loading among the army personnel followed by some rapid movement to the rear toward Hungnam. We paid them no further notice because we had no idea what that was, and we also didn't know what was going on with several drums of boiling water.

We were told that a field kitchen was coming up to serve us dinner to celebrate the Marine Corps birthday, and this was great news since we hadn't had a hot meal since Wonson. It was now November 10, and sure enough, here they came. We were given the word that half of us were to stay on the line and the other half were to go and get our chow. Boy, did they outdo themselves. There was hot turkey, dressing, mashed potatoes, cake, coffee, and nuts. And even though the food was cold, it was great. When you dipped your tray in the fifty-five-gallon drums of boiling hot water and walked about twenty feet to the chow line, the water on the trays was already solid ice.

The next day, our supply sergeant cleverly discovered (ha) some cold weather gear, including parkas, boots, and gloves, and we didn't ask where they came from. My parka came well below my knees, and my shoe packs were a size 11W even though my shoe size was 8. But that was all right because it left room for lots of air to circulate in the boots. It was like walking on snowshoes. Thank God I had eight pairs of socks to take up some of the slack. Boy, it seemed like we were really living now, first a hot meal and then cold weather clothing.

By the time we arrived in Chunghung-Ni area, we had been in combat for about three months since landing at Incheon, and no matter how disgusted or "teed off" about anything that had happened, I always tried very hard never to show any concern or a sign of emotion.

An army 155 mm artillery battalion moved into our area and asked for our support, and of course we said yes. We noticed that they had their own field kitchen and they said they would feed us. Talk about good luck for Charlie Company; Thanksgiving was right around the corner, and we were now going to get another hot meal with all the trimmings. The temperature was now around minus forty degrees and the wind was picking up. This was the cold air coming out of Siberia that would cut right through to the bones. Thank God our pup tents had snow covering them because it gave us a sort of insulation. This reminded me of the times back in Buffalo, when we would go camping with the Boy Scouts and when I learned how to keep warm. It sure helped me in the freezing cold of Korea.

We found out that by placing our canteen next to our body, it helped to stop the water from freezing. We were told to place the canteen along with our foot insole to dry and keep warm. This worked for a while until the temperature went down to minus thirty-five degrees. Then everything froze and we were back to eating snow. Life was miserable and morale was very low. But we looked at the big picture; we were still alive, and times would get better.

On the way out of the frozen Chosin, we had a WWII Chinese Marine in our squad. His name was Old Man Clark (he was over thirty-five years old). We were passing a bunch of Chinese prisoners, when one of them cried out Clark's name. Clark approached him and said, "Blanko, what are you doing here?" He was given the name of Blanko while he was Clark's house boy in Singtow, China. (The name Blanko was a cleanser that the Marines cleaned their leggings with and was given to the house boy.) When Clark asked Blanco what he was doing in North Korea, he stated that when the Marines left China in 1949, and after Chang Ki Check was chased out and went to Formesa, China, the Chinese Communist Army captured all the Chinese working for the Marines, gave them the option of joining the Chinese Army or being shipped off to the POW camps. He had no choice but to join the Communist Army. He was glad that he was captured because he knew that the Marines would take care of them. Clark was glad to see him and told him that the Marines would feed and give them warm clothing. That was the last time Clark saw him.

Charlie Company.

Death stare.

Under attack.

On the move.

Hoping to heat up some C rations.

Moving KIAs.

Moving Marines for burial at Koto-Ri.

US Army group that was ambushed and killed.

Heading south.

Still moving south on the long, steep, winding road.

Marines killed in action, clothing removed by Communist Chinese.

One more day…

Ten-minute break, Ken Santor (far right).

Attempting To Keep Warm While Not Moving And Getting Some Much Needed Rest.

On the way out of Chosin, escaping to the Sea.

CHAPTER 13

FUNCHILIN PASS

At 0400 the next morning, Charlie Company led off for the First Battalion, up the steep winding road toward the Funchilin Pass in total darkness in a driving snowstorm that was bordering on a blizzard. The road turned back and forth like the famous Burma Road, and visibility was nonexistent. Our only maps were poor copies of unsatisfactory Japanese maps with no writing or symbols of any kind in English. The only way we could identify a village on the map was a small cluster of Japanese symbols crowded together. After following the road through several climbing turns, we were scheduled to leave the road and climb up the steep hill to our right. This to me was the worst mountain to climb because it was one step forward and two steps back, and to this day I can't remember how I carried our gun up this rotten mountain. It took forever to reach a small saddle at the top. The snow was coming down quite hard now, and the wind didn't make it any easier. Once we reached the top, we were to let Able Company pass through us and continue the attack toward the Funchilin Pass. Incidentally, all the above was to be accomplished during the hours of darkness.

The move along the road was slow and difficult in the darkness, but nothing compared to the climb up the hill above us. It was so steep that much of the time we had to use our hands to pull ourselves and each other up the hill. And again, we seemed to slip back two steps for every one we took due to the ice and snow covering everything. I should also mention the temperature was well below zero.

When daylight came, I was amazed to learn that in the darkness, we had gone up the hill too far north, and Charlie Company had secured Able Company's first objective without a shot being fired! The enemy had been unable to see us in the snowstorm and darkness, and the entire company always moved as quietly as possible so they couldn't hear us either.

The Chinese had large forces dug into the Funchilin Pass in blocking positions, to prevent other elements of the First Marine Division from moving back to the south toward Hungnam and Hamhung. When Able Company passed through us all hell broke out, and they were in a fierce firefight for most of the morning, with their wounded moved back over the hill with us. Able Company did a great job in eliminating them in an extended firefight before the first friendly element arrived from Koto-Ri. At the same time, Baker Company covered the road winding up the pass itself and really provided excellent security for all our forces to the north and west of Charlie Company's position on the hill.

The next day portable bridges were dropped from helicopters to replace the bombed-out bridge in the pass. Shortly thereafter, other First Marine Division units began to pass through the First Battalion, First Marines lines. A couple days later, the rest of the division had passed, and we were ordered to disengage and follow them south. We were happy to hear this since we hadn't had any food for two days. One of our machine-gun squad members volunteered to climb back down the hill and bring back some C rations. We learned later that he fell on the way down and was airlifted back to Japan. The trip down was worse than the trip up the mountain.

It should be noted that numerous US Army units had also passed through Chunghung-Ni and Koto-Ri on the way north before the Chinese entered the war. As indicated earlier, many of these army units disintegrated and frequently abandoned their weapons and equipment. When Charlie Company brought up the rear of the division on the way south, we were always on the lookout to pick up anything we could use. We had arrived in Chunghung-Ni with two jeeps and trailers that we had been issued months before. By the time we arrived on the bank at Hamhung, we had seven jeeps and trailers, two half-ton six-by-six trucks, and a weapons carrier—all this with US Army markings.

A few words about the weather we encountered while on the hills over the Funchilin Pass when the weather had really turned cold. By the first night we were in position, we were in the midst of a blizzard with winds in excess of fifty knots, and the temperature had dropped to minus thirty to forty degrees below zero Fahrenheit. The deep snow was drifting constantly, and in our exposed position, the cold was brutal.

One of the biggest problems we faced was with our boots. We had been wearing normal boondockers and leggings since landing at Incheon, but a few days before reaching Chunghung-NI, we were briefed by an army master sergeant who was a cold-weather expert on what to expect during periods of extreme cold. A few days later we began to receive a few shoepacks, but none of the insulated insoles that are worn with them. The problem was shoepacks are not satisfactory even with the insoles, which were not received in significant numbers. In fact, we didn't receive enough insoles for everyone until long after we went south to Hamhung. By the time we reached there, my feet were covered with blood and looked like hamburgers, just like most of the rest of Charlie Company. As I recall, the boots that had been designed for extreme cold didn't reach Korea until the following winter, long after most of us went home. While we were dug in on the hill near Funchilin Pass, the entire hill was covered with ice and snow, so we had to be very careful walking around.

A couple of days later, the units of the First Marine Division to the north of us began to leave Koto-Ri, across the bridge which had been installed over the gap in the Funchilin Pass, and they passed through our position. We were happy to see old friends coming through, and we helped them the best that we could. It took the rest of the division several days to pass our lines on the way to Hamhung. We were ordered to remain in place and protect the rear of the division, so we became the last battalion (and company) to return to Hungnam.

After walking more hours, we were met by a column of six-by-six trucks which took us to Hungnam, to an area where the army had set up row after row of tents for the First Marine Division units returning from the Chosin Reservoir area. We were very glad to see them since they gave us a chance to thaw out for the first time in weeks.

Colonel Lewis "Chesty" Puller was known for leading his men from the front line and inspiring heroic actions. He was over fifty years old when he took part in the September 1950 Battle of Incheon Landing, as commander of the First Marine Regiment. Puller led his men fearlessly as the UN forces, that were made up of mostly Americans advanced north, following the retreating North Korean People's Army. By December, they were near the Chosin Reservoir when People's Volunteer Army of China poured over China-North Korean border and surrounded the UN Army. When Puller was updated about the dire situation, he said, "We've been looking for the enemy for some time now. We've finally found him. We're surrounded. That simplifies things." His Marines managed to keep the supply lines open, and they also acted as the rear guard during the withdrawal. They destroyed seven of the enemies' twenty-five divisions and inflicted heavy casualties on the rest. Puller was awarded his fifth Navy Cross for extraordinary heroism during the operation, which was the most of this award presented to any Marine in US history.

General O. P. Smith was never credited for his brilliant plan to save the First Marine Division from the attack by the People's Volunteer Army of China. It was known by the men of the First Marine Division that this was a big mistake, and that Chesty and General O. P. Smith were overlooked by the higher-ups. We all believe that to this day, they should have both received the Congressional Medal of Honor.

On the way out from the Chosin Reservoir, over one hundred thousand North Korean civilians had decided that they had had their fill of communism, and they decided to follow the Marines out of the Chosin. They were later put on ships and transported to Pusan, South Korea, along with the Marines. They left North Korea with everything that they owned, which was very little—literally only the clothes on their backs.

When the North Korean civilians returned to South Korea, they were met by family members that were separated when the Russians took over the north at the end of World War II. I have always wondered what happened to these people. Did they really give up the communist way of life for the chance to travel south?

There is another Marine I would like to talk about. His name was First Lieutenant Kurt Lee, a World War Two Chinese American who served in the Seventh Marines. Those in command gave him the task of leading relief Marines high in the ridges of North Korea, to bring support to Marines that were outnumbered by the Chinese. His job was to lead his men in total darkness, in snow up to two-feet deep and in subzero-degree temperatures. While suffering from gunshot wounds, he lead his Marines to help the surrounded Marines and was later given the Navy Cross to keep him quiet about his deeds. There was no way they were going to give a Chinese man the highest award. We still believed that if you did not belong to the "good old boys club" you were out in the cold.

I had met First Lieutenant Kurt Lee at one of our "Men of Chosin" reunions, and we talked about the battles that were fought and how miserable we were. First Lieutenant Kurt Lee died all alone in his apartment with no one there to help him. Rest in peace, First Lieutenant Kurt Lee. Please keep those gates guarded for the rest of the Chosin Few. We know the truth.

Another notable personality to mention was Marguerite Higgins, who was born in British-controlled Hong Kong on September 3, 1920, and she died on January 3, 1966, at the age of forty-five. She was the only child of Lawrence Daniel Higgins, an American who served as a pilot in World War 1, and Marguerite Goddard, a French woman he had met while in Europe.

I met Marguerite on the outskirts of Seoul, in September 1950, and for some reason she felt very comfortable with Charlie Company, and it was the same for photographer David Douglas Duncan. Both were war correspondents, and they both covered World War II, Korea, and later Vietnam. They covered most of Charlie Company's daily action in the south, and Marguerite was a very good sport, sleeping in a tent and eating C rations like the rest of us. After we secured Seoul was the last time we saw of her until December 1950, when we were on the way out of the frozen Chosin. Somehow, she was able to sneak into the midst of hostile action with the Chinese, south of Koto-Ri in North Korea.

It was many months later that she showed up at the Chosin, when Chesty heard that she somehow convinced someone to take her where the action was. Chesty said in so many words to "Get that woman out of here, like, right now."

When she was being driven out, she stopped to talk to a Marine who was walking south. She asked the Marine what he would remember the most in years to come. "Well," he said, "I guess the most important thing that I can remember would be pulling a three-inch pecker out of six inches of clothing to relieve myself." She said thank-you and jumped back into the jeep and headed south.

IN HER "WORKING CLOTHES" AS A WAR CORRESPONDENT IN KOREA, MARGUERITE HIGGINS STILL MANAGES TO LOOK ATTRACTIVE

GIRL WAR CORRESPONDENT

Photo from October 1951 *Life* magazine article by Carl Mydans.

Boarding the ships with one hundred thousand North Koreans.

Second Lieutenant Henry A. Commiskey

Lieutenant Commiskey was no stranger to war. As an enlisted Marine he had been wounded at Iwo Jima and received a letter of commendation for "exhibiting high qualities of leadership and courage in the face of a stubborn and fanatical enemy."

Born in Hattiesburg, Mississippi, in 1927, he had joined the Marine Corps two days after his 17th birthday. He served more than five years as an enlisted man and was a staff sergeant drill instructor at Parris Island when he was selected for officer training in 1949. He completed this training in June 1950. Two months later he was with the 1st Marines and on his way to Korea.

He came from a family of fighters. His father had been a machine gun instructor in World War I. One brother had been with the Marine Raiders in World War II. Another brother was badly wounded while with the 187th Airborne Infantry in Korea.

In the action on 20 September, that gained Henry Commiskey the nation's highest award for valor, he escaped unscathed, but a week later he was slightly wounded in the fight for Seoul and on 8 December seriously wounded in the knee at the Chosin Reservoir. Sent home for hospitalization, he recovered and went to Pensacola in September 1951 for flight training, receiving his wings in June 1953 and then qualifying as a jet pilot.

He returned to Korea in April 1954 as a pilot with VMA-212. Coming home in September, he returned to line duty at his own request and was assigned once more to the 1st Marine Division. Next assignment was in 1956 to Jackson, Mississippi, close to his birthplace, for three years duty as a recruiter. In 1959, now a major, he went to the Amphibious Warfare School, Junior Course, at Quantico, and stayed on as an instructor at the Basic School. He retired from active duty in 1966 to Meridian, Mississippi, and died of a self-inflicted gunshot wound on 15 August 1971.

Citation:

For conspicuous gallantry and intrepidity at the risk of his life above and beyond the call of duty while serving as a Platoon Leader in Company C, First Battalion, First Marines, First Marine Division (Reinforced), in action against enemy aggressor forces near Yongdungp'o, Korea, on 20 September 1950. Directed to attack hostile forces well dug in on Hill 85, First Lieutenant Commiskey, then Second Lieutenant, spearheaded the assault, charging up the steep slopes on the run. Coolly disregarding the heavy enemy machine-gun and small-arms fire, he plunged on well forward of the rest of

Department of Defense Photo (USMC) A43766

his platoon and was the first man to reach the crest of the objective. Armed only with a pistol, he jumped into a hostile machine-gun emplacement occupied by five enemy troops and quickly disposed of four of the soldiers with his automatic pistol. Grappling with the fifth, First Lieutenant Commiskey knocked him to the ground and held him until he could obtain a weapon from another member of his platoon and kill the last of the enemy gun crew. Continuing his bold assault, he moved to the next emplacement, killed two or more of the enemy and then led his platoon toward the rear nose of the hill to rout the remainder of the hostile troops and destroy them as they fled from their positions. His valiant leadership and courageous fighting spirit served to inspire the men of his company to heroic endeavor in seizing the objective and reflect the highest credit upon First Lieutenant Commiskey and the United States Naval Service.

CHAPTER 14

BACK TO PUSAN

On our way back to Pusan, I met a bunch of buddies that I had served with while in Baker Company, Fifth Marines. We talked about old times and about the friends that were wounded and the ones who went to heaven to guard those pearly gates. It was great seeing and talking with them.

Upon arrival in Mason, near the southern tip of the Korean peninsula, we went into reserve status, and this gave us a chance to thaw out and relax a little and get some replacements for our battle and frostbitten casualties. After a few days, we were ordered to have a battalion formation at which time Colonel Puller would award some medals. Following the ceremony, Chesty indicated he wanted to speak to the troops, so we went to "parade rest" and he sounded off. He congratulated us for the great job of fighting we had done and assured us that there would be plenty more to come. He then caught us by surprise. Referring to the M-1 and M-2 .30 caliber carbines, with which many of our officers and NCOs were armed and which were notoriously undependable, he stated, "You say you don't like damn carbines? Neither do I. The damned thing is they are no good, so throw it away and get yourself an M-1 or a BAR." When Chesty was out of earshot, our skipper said nobody was going to throw away any carbines, and that the first man to try it would probably be shot by his company commander.

Mason was far enough south for us to have no worries about security from enemy forces. Everything was relaxed and informal, with hot chow, tents, and a chance to take it easy. The boys sat around groups and talked and walked around the entire division area and some even went hiking. Some of them went out and went deer hunting and shot a couple deer, while some shot a few beautiful pheasants.

Guerrillas in Sudong

When we were told to secure our actions in Sudong, we were told by battalion to check out an area close by, as it seems that one of the local Koreans knew about a large group of North Koreans that were giving the army problems at night. Apparently, they were held up at a location close by.

When we arrived at the top of the hill, we could see many North Koreans far below. Our section leader told me to set up our gun and to adjust our sight to over 1,500 to 2,000 yards away. When we were ready, we were told to fire a small burst to check our sights. Our target was so far away, I could see them but could not see where my shots were hitting. My spotter got very excited and told me to continue shooting. My shots were spread out a good fifteen to twenty yards, and it was raining bullets. When we could see no more action below, we were told to cease firing and secure my gun.

Later that evening, we were told the body count was over 285 killed or wounded—not a bad day's work. Oh, and the army had no problems after that.

When we were in South Korea, on our "Operation Killer" mission, we were given a seven-day break. We were surprised that the army had set up tents with heaters. Well, one of our Eastern Marines suggested that we brew up some cherries that were given to us from the Air Force into cherry gin. Well, none of our western boys knew anything about brewing, so we let the guy from the east do it. First, we had to find a container to brew the batch. We found a ten-gallon Jeep water can with a caved in center that you could still see the tire marks of where it had been run over. Next, he added the cherries, and then put in ten pounds of sugar, shut the lid, and waited for nature to take its place. After a few days, I was sitting on the can with the members of our squad around the stove, when all of a sudden there was this loud bang, and our eastern Marine knocked me off of the can and rushed outside with it. When he opened the lid, a large surge of foam, along with the cherries, shot up in the air a good ten feet. Thank God, it gave us a warning when it popped out the crease in the can. We could just see the headlines, ten Marines wounded when their cherries they were using to make cherry gin blew up in their tent.

CHAPTER 15

TROUBLE WITH THE ARMY

During the time the First Marine Division was attacking north from Hungnam through Sudong and Chinhung-Ni, Koto-Ri and Haguru-Ri, and Yudam-Ni, the Eighth Army was attacking northward to the west of us. The only coordination between the Eighth Army and the Tenth Corps, of which the First Marine Division was the largest part, was via General MacArthur's headquarters in Tokyo, and that is another story. However, the fact remained that there was no direct communication between the two. When the Chinese entered the war, the Eighth Army effectively disintegrated and dashed madly to the rear in retreat.

Despite what had happened to the Eighth Army, the Tenth Corps Commander Almond ordered the First Marine Division Commander, General Oliver P. Smith, to continue to attack to the north. General Smith was a superb combat leader, and he realized that to carry out the corps commander's order would jeopardize the First Marine Division, and he refused to comply with it. He then ordered the First Marine Division to hold up and consolidate its elements, which were spread out from Chunghung-Ni to south to Yudam-Ni to the north. The First Marine Division then commenced an orderly move to the rear to avoid enemy forces getting behind us due to the situation that was created by the Eighth Army's withdrawal to our west.

A few comments about General O. P. Smith should be of interest. When he was in Hagaru and Yudam-Ni, he had a jeep with trailer and a driver. When the First Marine Division was ordered to head south, there were many casualties who were desperately in need of transportation for medical care and rehabilitation. Many were flown out of Hagaru on Marine, Navy, and Air Force transports, but all others had to be taken out on trucks and other vehicles. Rather than ride in his jeep, General Smith walked out with the rest of us, and put the maximum number of casualties on his jeep and trailer so they could ride most of the way to Hungnam.

After the First Marine Division came out of the Chosin Reservoir, you may have read that available ships were sent to Hungnam to evacuate us. This actually took place, but in no way were we driven out. We were packed like sardines aboard a variety of ships as they became available. After the First Battalion, First Marines arrived at the coast, we stayed there for a couple of days defrosting ourselves, and we picked up army trench coats for the entire company from a warehouse. Shortly before we got under way, we looked at the town north of the bay and all the buildings and warehouses were blown up to keep them out of the hands of the enemy. And to think I almost got shot trying to acquire a single pair of gloves.

Shortly after that, we upped anchors and moved out of the harbor and headed south. As we looked around the ship, it was supposed to have about 1800 enlisted on board. As near as we could determine, we had more like 7,000 to 7,200 men aboard. To say it was crowded was an understatement of the day. The enlisted quarters were filled to overflowing, and many of our NCOs slept in the passageways. Their being in the passageway had them in position to move up in the chow line, which was serving continuously, and since it took about seven hours to make the cycle, this technique actually worked out pretty well.

A few days later, the battalion moved up to Wonju in preparation for the commencement of Operation Killer. When we jumped off the next morning, our battalion moved out in a column of companies up the road in the valley north of Wonju with Charlie in the lead. I recall Lieutenant General Ridgeway who was the Eighth

Army Commander at the time, complete with a supply of his well-known hand grenades and an aide (a major) carrying a map case for him. As we moved out, one of our Marines that was carrying a fully loaded pack and equipment noticed that his boot was untied. As the Marine tried to lean over to tie the lace, General Ridgeway walked over and tied it for him, even after the Marine assured the general that he could do it. A photographer took a photo of the general tying the lace, and it made the newspapers in the states a few days later. However, I'm certain that he was just trying to help the Marine and had no intention of getting his picture in the paper.

The attack north of Wonju was made against resistance which, for the first two days, varied from light to moderate in intensity. On February 22, the First Battalion was attacking northward with Charlie again in the lead. Our immediate objective was a low hill that was about a half mile in front of us. Colonel Schmuck and the battalion headquarters were a quarter of a mile from where we were ordered to hold up.

There was a sizable enemy force rapidly approaching the hill in front and from the north, and it looked like they would reach the top of it before we did. This would obviously make our attack much more difficult and costly, so we were told to attack in a skirmish line, and we took off. After a hard dash up the steep hill, we reached the top and immediately set about getting security out on all sides in preparation for an attack by the enemy.

We had friendly air support on the station over us in the form of four Marine F-4U corsairs. In our frantic dash up the hill, we apparently overran our objective before the corsairs pilots expected us to do so. This resulted in the first corsair making a run on us as we were consolidating our positions. We were unaware that the pilot thought we were enemy troops on the hill until he dropped a napalm tank, which landed about twenty yards from my position near the crest of the hill. Fortunately, the tank did not strike anyone, and the napalm did not ignite, but some fifteen or twenty of us were literally splattered with the napalm as the tank burst, spreading it in all directions. I glanced up and saw the second plane just starting its run on us. I called out for a panel, and a Marine standing near me whipped

83

off helmet and jerked a small panel from the inside of his helmet and threw it to me. I spread it open and held it up in sight of the pilot of the plane in its run, and to put it mildly, I was rather relieved when he immediately pulled out of dive and ceased the attack.

The night of February 22 was spent in a battalion perimeter a few hundred yards north of the position mentioned above. The following morning, we were ordered to take a company-sized combat patrol into town for two reasons. First, we were to determine the strength and location of enemy forces in the area. Second, we were to attempt to locate some US Army survivors of an enemy attack of some weeks before ("Massacre Valley," Thirty-Second Infantry, as I recall) who were reportedly in hiding in the town and awaiting the return of US forces.

As we progressed across a flat and open area, we were taken under long-range enemy machine-gun fire from the hills to our left. The machine gun effectively pinned us down, and there was a call for our mortar section leader to come forward so we could point out the location where it was coming from. A few minutes later, we saw him approaching very nonchalantly, walking along with a blade of straw sticking out of his mouth. About twenty yards behind my position were a row of mud puddles. As he walked past, the heavy enemy machine gun opened fire on him, and I could see where the bullets were hitting the mud puddles about four feet apart and were rapidly catching up with him. I shouted to him to either hit the deck or run to my position. He glanced back, saw the bullets were closing on him, and just kept walking toward me saying, "No problem, they'll straddle me." He was right, the slugs missed him, and we figured he must have had more than one guardian angel looking out for him that day.

CHAPTER 16

THEY WON'T NEED IT ANYWAY

After about a month in Mason, we received some replacements, new weapons and equipment, and we were ordered to go by truck to the Andong-Uiseong area. While we were there, Charlie Company, reinforced with a battery of 105s from the Eleventh Marines, was sent on a three-day patrol to Samgori, a small town east of Andong. Intelligence reports advised us that there was a company of enemy forces in the area. We reached the outskirts of Samgori to set up our 105s and proceeded to clear the town of Chinese by fire and maneuver, supported by our artillery.

On the way back to our position in Uiseong, we drove through the Tenth Corps post area in Andong and parked for a short time in their motor pool. When we reached Uiseong, we returned to our earlier positions, set out our sentries, and turned in for the night. The next morning, an army military police officer drove up to our position and asked to see the company commander. He informed the skipper that after we left the Tenth Corps motor pool the day before, they found that they were missing a three-fourth ton weapon carrier and a jeep. The skipper told him that we did observe an overheated weapons carrier parked alongside the road between Andong and Uiseong the day before as we returned to Uiseong. (It was true. It was abandoned by our boys when it wouldn't run).

He then informed the skipper that he had retrieved the weapons carrier, and if he could recover the jeep by the next day, nothing would be said. Otherwise, it would result in an official investigation, and somebody would get in serious trouble. The skipper assured him if we located the vehicle, we'd inform him and get it back to him. As soon as he left, the skipper told Gunny Cory to stop the crew preparing the army jeep for repainting in Marine colors and not to proceed with forging new serial numbers on the engine. He then sent it back to the Provost Marshal in Andong with a note saying that he hoped it was the one he was trying to find. Nothing else was ever said about it, but I'm sure he knew that we had the jeep, and he was just trying to get it back to Tenth Corps without embarrassing the Marines. We really didn't need it, anyway.

CHAPTER 17

ORDERS TO GO HOME

We went back to our last position and were waiting for the new replacement Marines to join our company. George and I were at our gun site cooking rice, and I had secured a large can of cherries. Our plan was to cook the rice and then cover it with the cherries that I got from the Air Force in our last town.

Well, the rice was just about ready, when a runner came up and stated the skipper wanted to see me on the double. Now, what the hell, I wondered. Did Theriot tell the skipper I was going to kill him if he ever got us into another mess?

When I got down to the skipper's tent, he said, "Santor, get your gear together, you're going home."

"What?" I said. "But, sir, I want to say goodbye to my buddies." He said, "Now!" I said under my breath, "Screw you, asshole, I'm going to say goodbye to George and the rest of the machine-gun squad." So I climbed back up the hill to say goodbye, and I noticed that the rice was ready to eat, so I sat down and had a bowlful with my squad and said my goodbyes. I told them that I'd make sure to send them some food and booze when I got home. Before I left, I gave George my .45 caliber pistol and binoculars and most of my clothes, seeing I would not need them now. George and I go way back to boot camp back in 1948, and I sure would miss him.

I reported to the skipper's tent and was told to board the truck that would take us back to the rear area. On the way out, we started to receive small arms fire; not having a weapon, I asked the truck driver if he had any. "Yes, there is a machine gun." When I picked it up, he asked if I knew how to use it. "I sure do," I said, "I'm a gunner." With that, I grabbed the gun and sat it on the truck's cab, which was a canvas cloth. The tripods went right through the cover. Just about that time, a company of Marines came over the hill and took care of the sniper.

When we arrived at the dock, we were told to board, and that we would stop first in Yokosuka to pick up some wounded and then proceed to Kobe, Japan, to get our seabags. While in Yokosuka, Japan, we were treated to a steak dinner, I think this was where the first "steak on a hot skillet" came from; it was steak, French-fried potatoes, veggies, and all the milk we wanted.

When we arrived in Kobe, I was amazed on how fast they located our seabags because I was sure mine was lost, but it wasn't.

We then boarded our ship to return to the USA, I remembered how boring it was when we got on the ship coming over, and I didn't want that to happen again. The first thing I asked was, "Can I volunteer to do something on the ship to pass the time?" They asked how I would like to work with the ship's baker, and I said sure, so I did this for ten days, working nights in the galley baking sweet rolls for breakfast and sleeping all day.

We finally arrived in San Francisco. The Marine band was there to greet us along with a large group of people. News reporters came on board to interview some Marines, but I avoided them because I wanted to surprise my family. We disembarked from the ship, got into private convertible vehicles, and went downtown San Francisco, where the mayor gave us the key to the city.

We got on buses and were transported to Treasure Island, and upon arriving, we were escorted to our quarters. They then informed us to meet at the sick bay where a corpsman gave us paper cups and told us to deposit a stool, so they could check everyone for pinwheel worms. Well, it turned out that we all had them and don't ask me how we got them. I never ate anything but GI food. We were all given pills the size of quarters.

After three days of testing, we were released to go on liberty. Cruze was my buddy who had a girlfriend who lived in San Francisco, and they wanted to fix me up on a blind date, so I said sure, that was all right with me. I was told to meet up with him on the corner and wait for them to return with my date. As I was standing there, a very well-dressed older gentleman came up to me and asked if I was on the ship from Korea.

I said yes and that I waiting for my friends to pick me up. We chatted for a while, and he said, "Do you know who I am?" I said, "No, sir, sorry, I don't." He walked over to a newspaper stand, pulled out a newspaper, and said, "This is me." I looked at him funny, like, is this guy nuts. I had no idea. He said, "I like you, come on with me and I'll buy you a drink." I said "Sorry, sir, but if I leave this corner, my friends will think I got cold feet and left." He said again, "When I tell people who I am, they fall all over themselves and try to kiss up. You know what, after you get home and visit with your family, call me and I will arrange to have you picked up and you can spend some time at my home, it's off Highway 1 in Big Sur." About that time, my friend drove up, so I said goodbye and got into their car and drove off. Once in the car, they asked me who that man was, and when I said I don't know, they said he owned the newspaper that he was holding. *Oh my god*, I thought, *that was Randolph Hearst who owned the San Francisco newspaper*. I told them about him offering me to spend time at his home on Highway 1 in Big Sur. Again, oh my god, that is the San Simeon Castle, and he invites no one. You must have made a good impression. I said, "I just acted like myself," and had to say that I've not been known to be impressed with people or money. We had a good time that night, and I kept thinking, maybe I should have at least gotten his phone number.

Checking back in at the base, and after a few more trips to sick bay, I checked out with the corpsman and got paid for the first time in nine months. I packed my gear and went to the Greyhound bus station for my trip home. I was really looking forward to going home to see my family. Well, the trip took longer than I thought, but I guess I was just excited to get there. We arrived in Los Angeles early next morning, and I made a phone call to my family. They were very excited to hear from me; they didn't even know if I was on that ship. The papers didn't list the names of the Marines for some reason, and

I told them that I was at the Greyhound bus station in downtown Los Angeles, and I would be in the diner having breakfast with three of my Marine buddies.

Later a man came into the diner and called out my name. It was my father, and after we greeted each other, I introduced him to my Marine friends. I started to reach into my pocket to pay for my meal, and Cruze said, "Don't worry, it's covered," and we left. When we got to the car, my mother jumped out and hugged me and started to cry, saying she thought we would never see me again after the newspapers printed that the First Marine Division was surrounded and trapped at the Chosin, and they didn't think we would survive. Also in the car was my little sister Elizabeth who greeted me with a big hug. I told Elizabeth I brought her a present from Korea. It was a sterling silver ring, taken off the finger of a North Korean who tried to kill me, but I got him first.

When we finally arrived home, there were my twin sisters, Jimmy, Danny, and Louis, whom I later called Huey, Louie, and Dewey. I also noticed how big they had gotten. Our mother cooked a very large breakfast for all of us, and our father said, "See you all later, I have to get to work." I was so very tired. I went to bed and fell into a deep sleep.

The next day we went to see my Aunt Josephine at her restaurant to meet all my aunts and uncles. After we all hugged and said hello, and everyone started to get emotional. My Uncle Mike was my favorite, and Uncle Frank and Uncle Tony were there too and said that they were glad to see me and that they were too old to serve again. And of course, they said again, "You should have joined the Air Force and you would not have gone through all that hell." I stated that they were right and that the Marines truly did spend our day in hell.

That twenty days of leave went by so fast, and then I had to report back to Camp Pendleton. I was placed in the special service battalion and was asked if I would like to be reassigned to my old job at the northern patrol sector with the military police unit until they could find me a permanent job. I said that I would like that, so I stayed with the military police at San Onofre for a few months.

Then one day, our captain called me into his office and said there was an opening at the rifle range. They were looking for a Marine who had served in Korea with combat experience to train replacement Marines who would be going to Korea to fight. I took the job right away, packed my gear, and they took me to the rifle range.

When I got there, I was introduced to the gunner who ran the range and the three other Marines who worked and lived there, so I moved in. My jobs were to set the ammo on the range for the day of firing and to coach Marines on how to set their sights, hold their breath, and squeeze the trigger and fire. A lot of the young Marines had never fired a Garand M-1 rifle, and they were told not to jerk the trigger, just make sure to hold it tight into the shoulder and it will be all right. They asked me about Korea, and I told them to thank God, because they now had come out with cold weather gear, and they would never have to go through what we did. I also told them, "Here on the range, we teach you how to sight, breathe, and squeeze the trigger, but in combat you don't have the time to follow what we teach you. You sight your target and fire and kill or be killed." They also asked how I survived, and my response was that my guardian angel worked overtime, and that God had other plans for me.

I stayed at the range until my enlistment was up, and when they asked me if I would like to ship over and reenlist, my response was no because I had to get on with my life.

I was discharged on February 5, 1952, which was about year over what I had signed up for, since President Harry S. Truman gave all of us one extra year due to the on-going Korean war. I was paid my last pay, said goodbye to my fellow Marines, and left.

CHAPTER 18

MY NEW LIFE AS A CIVILIAN

I was discharged on a Friday and told my parents that I was going to take it easy and maybe go somewhere to relax. I was wrong, because on the following Sunday evening, my Uncle Mike called and said that he was in bed with the flu. He had to be on the job on Monday, but he wasn't going to make it, and asked me if I would do it for him. Uncle Mike was an electrical contractor, and he wanted me to show up for the job. I told him that I didn't know the first thing about electrical work, but he said that that would be okay and that I just needed to show up. Well, so much for my plan to do nothing for now. Little did I know that this would be my life's work for a very long time.

After he got back on his feet, Uncle Mike called and wanted me to go to work with him, and I did. I went to electrician apprentice school for four years, and then left him and went to work for another electrical contractor. I stayed with him for over four years and joined the union, which turned out to be something of a hassle.

I worked eight hours a day while going to night school on my GI benefits. I did this for over two years and decided that the trade I was pursuing in the television field did not pay very well, so I quit night school and decided to be an electrician. The pay was much better and had a better future for me.

When the family was living in the old home, I decided it was too small and so we moved to a larger home in a better neighborhood, because it was closer to the school for my sisters and younger brothers. I continued to work during days and go to school during nights, and this lasted for over two years. One night, when I was returning home, I noticed a young lady cutting flowers in the dark with a flashlight, and when I asked her what she was doing, she said that she was doing this so that she could meet me. Every night she would sit by her window and wait for me to come home. Little did I know, she was the girl I had dreamed about when I was in Korea. We started dating, and this went on for about three years, while I went to night school at Glendale College, and I was taking a course in gemology. We would go on road trips with my 1941 Ford Jeep, and we had lots of good times. Finally, I asked her to marry me. I sold my jeep to purchase her ring, and every time I saw her, I would think about my jeep. It was worth it because I was in love for the first time in my life. After we got married, I purchased a home on my Cal-Vet Loan. It was only 925 square feet with two bedrooms, one bath, and a one car garage. After our honeymoon, I went back to work for one year, and then decided to take the electrical contractor license exam. I passed it and sold my car to start my business with the money I got from the car.

I was lucky because I got a job wiring a tract of new homes, and my brother Albert helped me to do the work. About one year after I started working as an electrician, my wife Anne told me that she was pregnant. I was so delighted and happy about this. When little Ken was born, we were so excited. My father and the three younger boys came to visit since they were now uncles and they wanted to see our new son.

We had decided that our home was too small, so we were going to move to a larger home. My GI loan for our first home was for $9,500 and our payment was $45 a month, which included interest, insurance and taxes. But now our new home was purchased with my GI insurance and the new payment was $85 a month, and I was so worried about how I was going to afford it.

We moved to a small town called Sunland, and this home was 1,200 square feet and had a swimming pool. Everything was going well because I had quite a few jobs in Glendale, which was fifteen

93

miles away, where most of my jobs were. It was then that Anne told me she was pregnant again, and again we decided that our home would just be too small. We started to look for homes in Glendale and found a hillside lot for $5,000, so we bought it and started to design our new home. It would have three bedrooms and a total of 3,000 square feet. I built the home for a total of $21,000 and the mortgage payment would be $220 a month. Wow, how would I pay for this, I worried. The home was finished, with no furniture except for our beds and a few other items. For about three years, since there was no such thing as credit cards back then, everything had to be paid for in cash. Little Suzanne was born while the construction was going on, so the house had to be finished as soon as possible.

My jobs were becoming plentiful, and it started to get to the point where I needed help to keep up with the work. I rented a small shop in Glendale and added a light fixture service and installation to my business as the business grew, and I had to hire more help to keep up. As my company's name got more well known, I started to go after commercial and industrial jobs to add to the services I could perform, since they were more complicated and rewarding. I decided to get out of the residential housing market and concentrated on my new venture, which was doing city and government jobs. The pay was better, and I didn't have to worry about collecting on the smaller jobs to run my business.

I started to contract with JPL, which was a government backed company with projects that involved wiring a new building for the Mars launch. After this was done, I moved on to other jobs. We started to visit Lake Tahoe for vacations, and we liked it so well that we purchased a cabin in Incline Village. We would take weekends and long weeks at the lake, and it got harder and harder to go home to Glendale. We would visit Reno on holidays and enjoyed it very much.

One morning, at 6:00 a.m., we were awakened by bulldozers that were cutting into new lots above our home, and so we decided to move to Nevada. Glendale was getting too big, and crime was happening every day. My wife had gotten hold of a newspaper from Reno, Nevada, and she saw a home for sale. She contacted the real estate broker and made an appointment to see the house. We flew up to Reno and saw the home, then went home and talked about it and decided to buy it. We then put our Glendale home up for sale, and it sold immediately for $180,000.

Our move to Reno was arranged as soon as escrow closed. Just like that, we started to pack, hired a moving company, and moved to Reno. I then started to wind down my electrical and general contractors' business.

This was something new for my wife, and as she grew socially. She met other women and started to join clubs. This was something she could never do in Glendale because all her friends belonged to clubs that she could not join. She got involved in the Reno Chamber Orchestra, the Lady's Guild, and other nonprofit groups. For me, I concentrated on remodeling our new home, which took about a year. After this she said to me, "You know, you are starting to get on my nerves."

After she told me that, I decided to get involved in some new gas and oil ventures. I went to Texas, met with a land agent, bought some leases, hired an oil geologist, and started to drill my first well. The first well came in as a gas well, and since it was common to name wells, I named it after my wife and called it Annabelle 1. There would be two more wells with her name. After I secured a second lease and drilled my fourth well, it came in as a small oil producer, and this well was named after my daughter, it was called Suzanne 1. Then there was a second well that was called Suzanne 2. After acquiring and drilling five wells, I continued to purchase three more wells and then built a gas line to market the gas. This gas company was for sale under a court order to pay off their bills, and it went up for auction. On the day of auction, there was only one other bidder in attendance, so I won the bid and acquired a pipeline that ran over five miles, which included lines that went under major highways. I then secured other producers to sell and transport their gas and things were going very well.

My Texas land man was Donnie Smith, who lived in Talpa, Texas, which was about twenty miles from Abilene, and we became good friends. He lived with his mother who was a retired schoolteacher, and they lived on a section of land that had been given to their great-great-grandfather Josey Beal by the Spanish through a land grant. Not only was I associated with a long-time Texas family, we became good friends and things were looking great.

Things were going well when all of a sudden, my wife passed away in 1981. This was a blow I wasn't expecting, and I was very heartbroken and lost all my dreams. I could not function for over three years, and I sold everything that my wife and I acquired over the years, including our home in Incline, Nevada, our Levi's store business, and condos in Kauai, Hawaii. I lost all interest in everything we had.

It was 1984, and I was so bitter about life in general, and then one day I remembered about a time when my wife said that I should think about running for office. I remembered thinking that I could not run because I didn't know anything about politics. She had said that since I was a veteran that it should count. It was not time for state elections, but there was an opening for Nevada State Treasurer at the time, so I applied and started my campaign. I was completely unknown, but I ran and lost to a well-known woman by a few votes. Then in 1987, I ran again and won in every county and was elected Nevada state treasurer. I was still angry about losing and decided to take it out on our state representatives and state senators. I ran my office like a business and succeeded in breaking every state record in investments and introducing new ways for the office to invest. The office made over $200 million in interest on investments. I even made more money than the previous two state treasurers together. I was given the job of organizing the Nevada state payroll, and my office was writing over $35,000 checks every two weeks, which is a job that the state treasurer does to this day. I was the first state treasurer to balance the books for the first time since the office was started. And I successfully built a solid foundation for other state treasurers to follow.

In 1989, the Nevada legislature passed a law to build a veteran's cemetery in Clark County, and I thought that if Clark County had a cemetery, then northern Nevada should have one also. They then amended the bill so that northern Nevada would also have one built.

The government put up the money with a stipulation that we would have two years to build it, or the money would revert to them. One year passed, and I checked with the architect to see how the plans were coming, but the architect said he hadn't started on them yet, and that the senator and assemblyman were dragging their feet on this. I was very angry, because if we didn't build it in two years, we would lose the funds and would probably never have the opportunity again to build a cemetery. I met with our chief reporter in the capitol and told him about this and he put it in the paper. This angered the senator and assemblymen, and they were going to get me for this, threatening me with impeachment and other things. I put an ad in the paper for all the veterans in Nevada to mail in $5 to help with the projects. Both cemeteries were built on time, but they said that the punishment for my actions would be that my name would not be included on the plaque to be placed at the cemetery. I couldn't have cared less because I got them built and that's what mattered most.

It turns out that things didn't end there, as they accused me of making illegal investments, not running my office as the Nevada constitution stated, and that I didn't know what I was doing. Even though the investments were those chosen by every other state treasurer in the country, there was never legal documentation for this. I checked with every state treasurer to give me a copy of their legal opinion, but no one had one. Along with the state attorney general, we penned a legal opinion, and this became law. They even threatened me with withholding their approval of my budget, but I didn't need their budget, and I could generate my own funds to run my office. They really did not like this but ended up finally approving my budget. They even called me "a screw ball," and I eventually went ahead and got a legal opinion on new investments for all future treasurers to use.

It was now 1990, and with my term ending the following year, I decided that I would run again for this office. I enjoyed the treasurer job very much; in fact, it was the best job I ever had. Apparently, the powers that be didn't like me, and they ran a fellow Republican against me, but he was unknown in the state. There was a parade in Fallon, and when the parade was over, he and his wife, our lieutenant governor, and three others took off in his airplane. The airplane could not gain altitude and the plane crashed, killing his wife, and breaking the back of the lieutenant governor. On the next day, the newspaper ran the story in bold print, and I was defeated. Talk about a "silver bullet" and a message to me that said, "Get out of politics."

While I was the Nevada state treasurer, I approached the legislators that were in session in 1990 about coining a $20 silver coin. This coin would be used as legal tender in Nevada only, to stop the California banks from moving money from Nevada banks for their use. If the coin was available for use only in Nevada, it would have no value in any other states, and it was a win-win proposition for the state of Nevada. This was because Nevada was the largest producer of silver of any state in the union. My idea was to mint $20 silver coins that would be sold to only Nevada residents for $20 each as legal tender. The cost to make the coin would be between $3 and $4 each, so selling the coins for $20 would have meant a profit for the state of about $16 per coin. My thought was that by using prisoners to mine, stockpile, and manufacture the coin would be relatively inexpensive labor, about $10 per hour, which would still mean a profit for the state. My request for the first minting of the coin was $10 million, since the coins would probably sell out in a very short time, especially in Las Vegas, at $20 per coin. Minting one thousand proof coins, which means that the coin is blemish free, and each of these would sell for $100 each as collector's items.

In the event that the federal government ordered Nevada to stop producing these coins, each coin then would increase substantially in value due to its rarity, even though there is nothing in the US Constitution that prohibits anyone from minting coins. This concept was very simple and basic and would have been so profitable for the state of Nevada, but the state legislators could not even take the time to consider the possibilities, and my idea was shot down due to their ignorance and short-sighted, selfish behavior. This was even more disappointing as the profits from the sale of the coins would have gone directly to helping the senior citizens of Nevada.

I also approached the legislature about many of the state agencies that were scattered throughout Nevada and located great distances from the state capital. I proposed to the leadership to fund the treasurer's office $10 million to build an office building that would house all the state agencies.

Each state office has a budget for rent, which would have been paid to the state instead of third party owners or landlords, so that these rental funds would be paid back to the state which would pay the building off in a much shorter time. Again the legislators denied this, and the reason was that it would create a hardship for individual property owners throughout Nevada. My point was that the state legislators should not pay the state's money to private individuals because Nevada funds should be dedicated to the citizens of the Nevada. It is the state treasurer's job to safeguard the state's money to make sure it is not supplementing income to private individuals.

Fallon fifth graders visit with the Nevada State Treasurer, 1990.

CHAPTER 19

WITHOUT A JOB

Now that I was unemployed, I had nothing to do, and I could relax. I joined the Carson City Marine Corps League Detachment and enjoyed going to the meetings. In fact, I became their first Life Member. On the night of a league meeting in Carson City, we had a terrible snowstorm, and I couldn't make it because of the bad road conditions. Bob Holtzer was a Reno member, and together, he and I decided to form our own Marine Corps League Detachment in Reno. I contacted the national headquarters for the paperwork, and after securing the members, we formed the Battle Born Detachment. Our detachment grew so fast, we had to find a home to conduct our meetings. Bob Holtzer was also at the Chosin, serving with Tank Battalion and was severely wounded, losing an eye. Bob never new why he survived, and I told him that God had given him the gift of writing poems so he should continue doing it.

Around this same timeframe, I noticed that the local Marine Corps League was not active in Devil Pups, which was an organization that was started by two former Marines in California for underprivileged boys aged fourteen to eighteen years old. These two Marines went to Marine Corps Headquarters and to the Marine Corps Commandant to state their case and were given the go-ahead to establish the outfit, using Camp Pendleton for their encampment. I contacted the Devil Pups headquarters in California about forming a local Devil Pups program. They gave me their approval, and my first group of boys were ready to go. The only problem was no transportation. It just happened that one of our members in the Battle Born Detachment had a van that would handle the boys for this trip. We had no driver, so I volunteered for this job. Since my sister lived in San Clemente close to the base, I could stay with her for the ten days of the camp. God was watching out for me again. The trip was great, and our boys took home most of the trophies. Times have changed, and now they are accepting girls aged fourteen to eighteen years old.

After forming the Marine Corps League Battle Born Detachment, I realized that there wasn't a Military Order of the Purple Heart in Reno. Again, I contacted the National Purple Heart headquarters office and inquired about forming a chapter in Reno. So here we go again, we ran an ad in our local newspaper looking for Purple Heart recipients, stating that we were going to form a chapter in Reno, and we were having a meeting. We had eighty-five people show up, and we formed the Military Order of the Purple Heart, Chapter 719, and I was elected its first commander.

Later on I was contacted by the national headquarters about going to Las Vegas because they had three chapters there. The Nevada state commander had passed away, and the three chapters were disbanded. In order to have a state commander, we would have to have at least two chapters to function as a state department. They asked me to reform the three defunct chapters, which I did, and they also asked if I would be the state department commander, where I served three years. After that, national appointed me to be the Region VI commander, which was another three years, logging over one hundred thousand air miles servicing these regions and covering California, Arizona, Utah, Nevada, Guam, and Hawaii. I have also traveled to the Philippines trying to recruit new members and went on to swear in the members of the Guam chapters along with eighty-eight associate members. Guam was my favorite chapter because the members were like family, attending Mass every Sunday.

After my time as the Region VI commander, I was then appointed to the National Legislative Committee. We were tasked with walking the halls of congress and personally visiting representatives and senators. Our job was to ask them to provide their support for our interests and matters that concerned veterans by introducing bills and getting them passed.

This committee's first priority was to ask the legislators to support our request to the Postal Commission to create a postage stamp to honor Purple Heart recipients. It took three years for us to get this passed. After that, we went back to the Postal Commission with the request to make the Purple Heart stamp a forever stamp, and this took another two years, but we did it.

Our next project was to introduce and pass a bill to increase the US Government's standard payment to a veteran's surviving spouse on the death of the veteran, from $10,000 to $50,000. We also asked to include payments to the veteran's surviving family members, funds for the education of the veteran's children, and additional supplementary income for surviving spouses. After it was introduced, it took three years to pass.

After all the time spent travelling to DC working on these issues, I was pretty much burned out, so I resigned from my position on the national committee. It was time to let someone else do the heavy lifting, and I remained active as the commander in the local chapter.

CHAPTER 20

BOB HOLTZER'S POEMS

Earlier I mentioned Bob Holtzer and his gift for writing poems, and how I encouraged him to keep writing his poems. Bob was very emotional and could not forget about the past to move on with his life. He had that syndrome about "why me." So again, I assured him that he had a job to do and that his works would never be forgotten. I stressed to him to make sure that his poems would have a copywrite, so that some bastard somewhere down the line could not use them as his own. It took some doing with this hard-ass Marine to convince him, and he finally agreed to do it. I also told him to put all his poems together into a book. I really liked Bob. And then there was Darrel Deal, who was an army veteran from Korea, who had really wanted to be a Marine. Every time these two would get together, there was trouble, but I enjoyed hanging out and traveling with them.

They are now gone, but I have great memories and will never forget the good times we shared. I will now include his poems with this chapter, and I know that you will enjoy them like I do, and cry like I do.

Semper fi, buddies. Remember, I'm not there to rescue you and Darrel, but we'll someday meet again, when you have guard duty on those pearly gates.

These are Bob's poems included in this book:

- Look Around and Remember
- Memorial Reflections

- Chosin Tribute
- Christmas Lost
- Hell Fire
- D for Dawg
- Angel's Gate
- Our Ship
- Mom
- Faces of America
- Lessons Learned
- Remember Me?
- Freedom's Ballad
- Hallowed Ground
- Rally Round!
- The Old Man
- The Breed (Heart of the Corps)
- Freedom's Call
- The Unknown

WORLD WAR TWO

WHAT A PRICE

THEY PAID!

FOR FREEDOM.

YOUR

FREEDOM,

"FREEDOM"

KOREA

VIETNAM

Written as a tribute to all who fought & died for freedom.
Dedicated to the forgotten war that was Korea.
(especially to the "Men of Chosin")
Robert C. Holtzer (U.S.M.C. Ret.)
One of the Chosin Few.

Look Around and Remember

Look around, look around, "What do you see?"
A sunny day with our flag flying free.
A sky of blue with the world at play.
Spring is here, "It's a holiday!"
Look around, look around, "What do you see?"
An old man and a child overlooking the sea.
They stroll on the beach in search of a shell.
This old man has lived in his own private hell.
His heart is heavy as he stares at the ground.
And he ponders his life as he looks around.
"Grandpa! Grandpa! There's a tear in your eye."
Yeah! You're right, son, and I'll tell you why.
Look around, look around, "What do you see?"
People at play and filled with glee.
Many years ago, when I was young.
I walked with "heroes," they died "with their songs unsung."
Look around, look around, "What do you see?"
The graves of these men that made us free.
"Look up there?" At our flag unfurled.
"These men died to save our world!"
"I look at you and what do I see?"
My youth in you, living life free.
I think of the price we had to pay and
My hope for you to my dying day
Are that you and my family will never know,
"The taste of war or wounds from a foe."
They say, "Goodbye," as he climbs the stairs,
He's resigned to the fact that "nobody cares."
Look around, look around, "What do you see?"
"Those men that died for liberty!"
Nah! It's spring and it's time to play.
It seems everyone forgot "it's Memorial Day."

Memorial Reflections

There were tears in their eyes as they stared at the ground.
As they prayed in silence, you could feel their hearts pound.
They looked at the statues through the sunlight's glare.
They said to themselves, "That's my buddy up there!"
Many years ago we were young without care.
We never dreamed of the battle we'd share.
"I miss you, pal!" You meant the world to me,
You saved my life, so I could live free.
The hardships and the sorrow we had to go through,
When the battle was over, "Why did God take you?"
They look around as they hear freedom's bell ring.
Their hearts feel empty, 'cause they can't change a thing.
They look at the statues of bronze and stone.
"That's my buddy up there!" But he's not alone.
No matter what battle was lost or won,
Our heroes will live in our hearts as one.
They paid a helluva price for you and me.
So we could come home and raise our family.
Now "Taps" is heard with the bugle call.
"These brave men died, they gave their all!"
The color guard fires a salute to the sky.
Why it was you and not me, "only God knows why!"

Chosin Tribute (1987)

Many years had passed,
It was now nineteen eighty-five.
We came to our reunion.
Just glad to be alive.
Soldiers, sailors, Air Force, and
Of course, the Marine Corps too.
We formed into a brotherhood
We called "The Chosin Few."
As we talked and reminisced,
We recalled the general's shout.
Surrender? Never!
"Retreat, hell! We're coming out!"
We rallied all together
Into a fighting team.
All to stand in battle,
Soldier, sailor, and marine.
"There are no enemy forces,"
Some trite official said.
"Well, let those politicians come
and count their dead."
Outnumbered by the masses
and surrounded every night,
We fought the enemy hordes
and prayed for morning's light.
Most of our weapons froze
As men fought and died.
Without food and sleep
Human comforts were denied.
A cry was heard, "I'm hit!"
"Oh god! What am I to do?"
"Hey! Don't worry buddy,
I'm staying here with you."
Life's not forever, so cheer up
And don't look so sad.

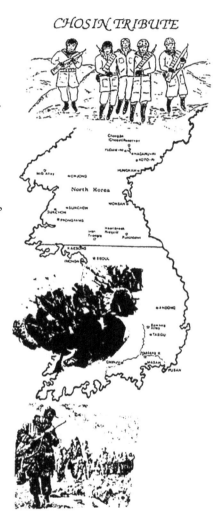

Compared to the cold at "Chosin,"
Hell can't be all bad.
The battle raged forever and
We made it to the sea.
"It would be known as an achievement,
If not a victory."
We wrote a page in history and
To the gory of the corps,
Those days hell did freeze over
"At Chosin Reservoir."
We gather here together
To pray and pay our due.
To pay tribute to our fallen,
Our brothers, "The Chosin Few."

THE TOOTSIE ROLL MARINES

Christmas Lost (1988)

As I lay there in the hospital and words were hard to find,
I'd been wounded in battle, and my wounds had left me blind,
In self-pity, I thought, "I'm blind! I'm blind!" I began to curse,
Then fate brought me some eyes in the shape of a nurse,
She asked, "How can I help you? Just tell me, what can I do?"
I said, "Act as my eyes and write, I have some words for you."
You know it's close to Christmas and I have a story to tell,
Send a letter to my dad, so I can tell him that all is going well.
"Dad, I've been hit, please don't worry I'm going to be okay,"
Don't let my little mishap spoil your Christmas Day.
Who knows? I might be home, but I'll never be the same,
There are men that died to save my life, "I don't even know their names."
They gathered all around me to form a protective shell,
You see they died to save me from "Korea's frozen hell."
Christmas is the birth of Christ, I'm told, the Prince of Peace,
Yet men die in war, please tell me why, "when will the bloodshed cease?",
I think of the past holidays and my world that used to be, you see.
Oh, Christmas will come again at home, but it will never be the same.
Til men can live their lives in peace, in the glory of "God's name."

111

Hell Fire

In the cold of winter, when the snow starts to fall,
My heart is filled with memories, I'd rather not recall.
Those days of my youth when I heard the battles roar.
In Korea's frozen hell at the "Chosin Reservoir."
"Hell Fire Valley," we were trapped with tank and truck
Hit with machine guns and mortars, at first we went amok,
Men falling in battle, I can still hear their cries,
Faces twisted in pain and terror glazed their eyes.
"Turn the trucks around!" I heard somebody yell,
I reached for my buddies, I watched them as they fell.
We rallied altogether to stop the enemy tide,
We prayed as we fought, "Dear God," be on our side.
They hit us from all sides, and they wouldn't let us rest,
Task force Drysdale fought on, and they did stand the test.
Bloodied and beleaguered, some men did make it thru.
To support the embattled bastion we called "Hagaru."
Those still on the road where the dead and wounded fell,
Were left to their fates, to spend a night in hell.
Our positions over run we felt the battles glare.
We crawled to new positions, but we found no help there.
Hit again, we shrunk into small circles to defend,
With the wounded and the dying, oh god! "Will it ever end?"
The battle was getting worse as it reached a fever pitch.
The enemy was killing our wounded as they fired into the ditch.
"Throw down your weapons? Surrender!" our tormentors cried.
"Stop and save your wounded, too many men have died."
"Go to hell!" they answered, as they fought on through the night.
"We've got to hold 'til dawn, cone on morning's light!"
They ran out of ammunition when they finally had to comply.
They'd surrender to save their wounded, "Please don't let them die."
They were marched off to prisons to suffer for many years.
I personally want to thank them "with all my heartfelt tears."

This tale of Hell Fire Valley may not seem much to you,
But those brave men of task force Drysdale "did help save Hagaru."
These men laid down their lives for the glory of the corps.
When we added to the "legacy" at the "Chosin Reservoir."

D for Dawg

They formed the Company D for dawg, a real raggedy crew,
Out of men of different backgrounds not knowing what to do.
Inexperience at first when duty gave them a call,
This hodgepodge of men would sacrifice their all.
Some went into battle not knowing their left from their right.
They would give their life for another in any given fight.
Hardship and sorrow was met with a "hardy cry,"
As these men of dog company would soon begin to die.
Faced with a massive enemy and Korea's freezing cold,
The young men of the company lost their youth and soon became "old."
Dog company lives in our hearts, remember one and all,
Pride and honor were written when we answered our nation's call.
D stands for dawg, we served during a time of strife.
When we answered duties call, "We lived a dawg's life."

Angel's Gate

Out here on the Pacific Coast, you can hear the ocean roar,
As the waves from distant oceans pound the Pacific shore,
Up here on the hill is a spot that lays in wait,
For a tribute to our fallen at a place called "Angel's Gate."
"Korea" was the war our nation soon forgot,
Except for us veterans, we vowed that we would not!
It was many years ago when we marched off to war.
None of us knew then what we were fighting for.
We fought for Korea's freedom to live another day.
But our own nation forgot our men, "the dead and MIA."
We will give a proper tribute to our friends from long ago,
This international memorial to those guys we used to know.
No longer to be forgotten and never again to wait,
Let's pay homage to our fallen at this place called "Angel's Gate."

Our Ship (1990)

As I gaze up at your proud and mighty bow,
My heart is filled with pride, "For many years from now,"
Men of great nations will hear your mighty "roar,"
as you sail on distant oceans to protect our nation's shore.
"With reverence," I think of the men you were named for,
that rag-tag group of survivors, from the Chosin Reservoir.
As you sail in harm's way…"Your colors will fly with pride",
In remembrance of our fallen, "All those men that died."
They will live on in you, "our ship," as you sail from shore to shore.
Your very presence will echo the saga of the "Chosin Reservoir."
This world has turned around from so many years ago,
You…"our ship" will send a message to let the whole world know,
"That men of valor"…still sail the seven seas,
Willing to sacrifice life…in the search for liberty.
"Sail on…mighty warrior! In search of lasting peace."
'Til the world can be free of war and all the bloodshed cease.

Mom

His mom had seen him off to war,
Today he came back home.
No more letters or cards would come,
All that had come to pass.
All that she would have to hold on to now was the flag,
With three pieces of brass.
Over the grassy knoll,
She heard "Taps" sounding its mournful cry.
A tear down her aging face,
As rifles pointed to the sky.
Piercing the silence came shot one, then two,
Then at last came three.
Then a silence came over this sacred ground,
As the flag was folded tenderly.
The three spent shells of shiny brass were buried inside the fold,
Then presented slowly to his mom, forever to have and to hold.
Holding it close to her heart,
She stood and walked across the grass.
While touching his casket softly,
She kissed the flag…with the three pieces of brass.

Faces of America

Because this nation was built by many races,
I am an American with many faces.
This land believed, where a man could be free,
Was built on the promise of equality.
In the thirties, refugees found this place to dwell,
From the haunts of prejudice from another hell.
In the forties, we fought a war for this just cause,
Men fought and died until victory was ours.
Then came the fifties when we thought the world was all right,
When the United Nations called us to Korea's fight.
"Vietnam" an action so misunderstood,
Now that peace has come to our home at last,
Do you think we've learned from the tainted past?
And salute our flag when it flies unfurled.
If we choose to let this world sail by,
The vanquished and defeated could be you and I.
Then this nation founded on freedom's ring
Would go to hell and not mean a thing.
Unless you and I can believe in our countries worth,
Then there will be no freedom here on earth.

Lessons Learned

Our country should learn this lesson well.
Before sending young men to another hell.
Patriots scream: "It's do or die!"
We've gone to war to that battle cry.
Europe was engulfed in a bloody snare,
We went to war to the song "Over There."
Men fought and died…"What did we learn?"
"The fact that freedom is hard to earn."
To live in peace for a little while,
How tranquil to see a loved one's smile.
How long it would last was hard to say,
Until December 7, "that infamous day."
Again we're engulfed in another war,
This time we knew what we were fighting for.
Our world as we knew it "proud and free."
Brave men would die for our liberty.
The fact that freedom is hard to earn.
Again we ask, "What did we learn?"
Korea faced the communist tide,
Most free nations went to her side.
The cry "to arms" was heard once more.
Again young idealists went to war.
Under one flag free nations stood,
In defense of freedom and for the world's good.
Questions were asked: "What's Korea for?"
"How can you win in a limited war?"
Our nation backed off and the die was cast.
Peace did come, but it wouldn't last.
The nation had some souls to sell and
They sent our men to another hell.
"Vietnam" in a world gone mad,
Our nation lost faith, "it was really sad."
Some people cried: "Hell no! I won't go!"
So we sent our best to face the foe.

Peace did come, "What did we learn?"
"The world's in ashes! Did you see it burn?"
Terrorists live and die by their guns.
"Dare we chance the loss of any more sons?"
We sit and ponder, we let the world turn.
Again that question: "What did we learn?"

Remember Me?

Overlooking the blue Pacific, there are statues that seem to wait.
Searching across the ocean for friends that were swallowed by their fate.
As the sun sets across the water and we end another day,
Just stop and think of our fallen, our dead and the MIA.
It was so many years ago when they were called to serve.
They fought and died, "our nation forgot." it's a fate they don't deserve!
It seems that on a clear day when I'm looking out to sea,
I feel I can hear their voices cry out: "Hey! Remember me?"
We're the fathers, husbands, and sons not remembered anymore,
We will never see our homes again or touch our nation's shore.
I thought I could forget the war from so many years ago,
But their voices tell me "don't forget" please let our nation know.
We fought to defend their freedoms, and we paid for it with our lives.
We will never know our homes again or families as husbands and wives.
Some of us had children, "we're the fathers they never knew,"
But we'd fight again to save them, "you know it's right to do."
As the night falls across the water and the tide flows out to sea.
Hear these voices that gave us freedom cry out: "Hey! Remember me?"

Freedom's Ballad (1986)

What a price they paid!
World War Two
Now that was quite a fight!
We went to war and what we did was right.
Men fought and died to end that strife;
And they all came home to a brand-new life.
But what a price they paid.
Korea came…we're in another fight.
Free nations defend, "Korea's right."
They hit Pusan! Again, Americans died.
Another war? Their mothers cried!
What a price they paid.
Incheon came…we crushed the enemy tide.
We pushed them back to the other side.
We thought we won! But the fates had lied.
What a price they paid.
The snow came down onto the valley floor.
In a mountain place called "Chosin Reservoir."
The enemy charged "Oh god, the guns did roar."
Men fought and died at Chosin Reservoir.
What a price they paid.
Outnumbered by ten to one and more,
"Hell froze over, Chosin Reservoir."
Survivors marched out,
"Their hands and feet were frozen."
From that day on they'd be "the men of Chosin."
What a price they paid. What a price they paid.
At Heartbreak Ridge, "The guns were smokin'."
At Pork Chop Hill, their hearts got broken.
Peace did come…but that was broken.
And Vietnam became another token.
What a price they paid.
And now my friends on some sunny day,
Think about…what they had to pay.

Another war? "A mothers cry!"
"Sons born to man,"
"So they could die?"
"What a price to pay."
What a price they paid for "freedom,"
Your freedom,
Freedom.

Hallowed Ground (1989)

Here in this earth we shall call "Hallowed Ground,"
We lay to rest the veteran, far from the battle's sound.
Born to this nation during its time of strife,
These men would value freedom more than their own life.
"They gave us today!" Our land that's proud and free—
These men would risk their lives to give us liberty.
They came home to a world that didn't know the score,
For many of our people would not go to war.
The price of freedom they didn't have to pay
Was bought and paid for by better men than they.
As we came to the end of life as all of us must do,
Be thankful to the veteran that sacrificed for you.
Freedom is not a gift that people should ignore,
The veteran bought and paid for it on many a distant shore.
As we pay homage—and words are hard to say—
Just think about these men and the price they had to pay.
"Rest in peace, old buddy!" Far from the battle's sound,
May you dwell with your God when you leave this "Hallowed Ground."

Rally 'Round! (1989)

Rally 'round the flag, boys? Was the cry our nation once heard.
In those days when men of honor fought for the expression of a word.
The flag, our nation's symbol, represents our freedom of speech.
In war, the banner of courage and commitment on many a foreign beach.
When our dead came home to rest in their beloved soil,
The flag embraced their caskets in remembrance of their toil.
I remember the parades of my youth when I stood free and proud
As the men we called patriots marched with the music blaring loud.
Today there is silence in our nation as we let our symbol die.
For the freedom of expression has changed as many years flew by.
There are those that express free speech in a manner of abuse.
They didn't buy that freedom or the right to its misuse.
They insult the heritage of this nation and the meaning of its worth,
With the abuse of this freedom they inherited only by their birth.
When duty calls to defend our freedom, I wonder where they will be?
Probably in a protest somewhere, while others die for their liberty.
"Rally 'round the flag, boys!" once again our nation's cry!
Don't let our flag be desecrated! Don't let our nation die!

The Old Man

In looking back to Korea, I can still see so many faces,
Of men we fought and served with in many different places.
We were strangers, when we first encountered the foe,
Pushed on by the courage of "the Old Man,"
The guy we called "CO."
The commanding officer, not many of us knew him very well,
But with his presence and experience, we'd follow him through hell,
I can still remember my first CO, before we hit the beach.
We attended Mass and a St. Christopher's medal came within my reach.
It was taken by another when I heard: "Here, take mine! I've got one,
    son."
It was the "Old Man," I never dreamed when it came to dying, he
    would be the one!
His replacement was with us when the battle ceased to roar.
He stayed to save the wounded, to become a prisoner of war.
The commanding officer? The old man? Remember him? You say?
"Yeah! I remember my commanders," those men gave me today.

In tribute and memory of L. B. Chase and H. B. Turner (D1 TKS).

"The Breed"
(Heart of the Corps)

The Breed (Heart of the Corps)

Look at them! Who are they? I'd really like to know.
These gallant young men that stand ready to defend and challenge
    our nation's foe.
You might ask this question when you come upon this scene,
When there's a crisis in our world and hope is dim just call on any
    "Marine."
It was "1775" when they formed into the corps,
To fight and defend our country on many a distant shore.
They fought in actions around the world, and they earned a new
    respect.
They served with pride and honor to become known as Leatherneck.
In World War One at "Belleau Wood" with a courage that few had
    seen,
They painted our history with valor, Devil Dogs, a name for a Marine,
In World War Two in the Pacific, they planted their courageous seed.
Then again in Korea and Vietnam to become known as The Breed.
It doesn't matter what action in which they may have served.
They are Marines, "The Breed," an honor well deserved.
In peace they carry the legacy of those that went before.
These young men are the "breed," the heart of the corps.

(1989)

Freedom's Call (1989)

The Land of the Morning Calm, known as Korea's other name.
Was devastated by war when the United Nations came.
Pushed from Seoul to Pusan with their backs against the sea.
Brave men of different nations would die for liberty.
Incheon was the key to halt this enemy tide.
Across the Han to Seoul "so many of us died."
Victory was in our grasp as we hit on "Wonsan's Shore."
We'd travel to "hell's own mountains" the Chosin Reservoir.
Faced with new enemies, the cold and hordes of commie reds,
This lost legion fought their way to Hungnam's engulfed beachhead.
In the spring a new offensive would show the UN's will,
But the battles raged on with every "sullen hill."
Names like Heartbreak and Pork Chop would become names of sorrow,
For those men that gave their all, "never to see tomorrow."
These hills of Korea, windswept with winter's song.
Tell tales of our dead, "they've been buried there too long!"
Today all seems forgotten by countries that we fought for,
Our own country said conflict, they wouldn't even call it "war."
Korea's free thank one and all.
Those men that answered fate, "when freedom came to call."

The Unknown (1993)

At the Punchbowl in Hawaii,
Where banners for heroes are flown,
There's a resting place, a plot of land,
Marked: "Korea…US Unknown."
People pass by without a tear, it's sad,
"They're so all alone."
For within this spot there are heroes;
The souls of our unknown.
They rest here together nameless,
Regardless of faith or race.
Known only to God; "Yet."
We veterans know their face!
Look around; you'll see them all battle,
They died to tell our story,
For without them we would not be here today!
To bathe in all their "glory."
They were there when we cried out yesterday,
They helped to ease our pain,
They rest here today so all alone,
Not one of us recalls their names.
These men were all our buddies!
They saved us many years ago,
True, we may not recall the names,
But their face…"We'll always know."
We pray they are at peace today,
Within this "hallowed ground."
For today without these nameless men,
World peace could not be found.
Clouds across the skies will shed their tears
in many a foreign place,
True! They're known only but to God,
But we veterans know their face.

Forgive our lack of memory for names and
the disregard we've shown,
But forever and a day we'll see your face;
"The face of our unknown."

Remember "The Forgotten."

1950 — KOREA — 1953

 54,246 Dead
8,177 M.I.A'S

"Whatever battle was lost or won,"
Our Heroes will live in our hearts as one.

Robert Chadwick Holtzer (October 19, 1932–March 23, 2011)

Robert Chadwick Holtzer, Sgt. USMC, Ret, passed away at
Saint Mary's Hospital on March 23, 2011, surrounded by his family. Robert (Bob) was born in San Francisco, California, to parents
Harold Emil Holtzer and Margaret Fuentes. He was second to the
youngest child of seven children. He is survived by his loving wife of
fifty-nine years, Bonnie; daughters Linda Haggans, Cynthia Bittner,

and Julie Williford; grandchildren Jeremiah Williford, Austin Schuler, Sarah Bittner, Donald Bittner, and Jillian Haggans; sister Asalena Campana; and numerous nieces and nephews. He graduated from Jefferson High School in Daly City, California, went on to business college in San Francisco and became an accountant and realtor. He played semi-pro football, became a black belt in judo, and coached PAL (Police Athletic League) Football for ten years. He started running with the Washoe Wacos and Silver State Striders here in Reno. He ran marathons in Hawaii, San Francisco, and Washington, DC.

Bob was an active member of the Men of Chosin, Chosin Few, Marine Corps League, Purple Heart VFW, and the Sierra Nevada Chapter 1 of Korean War Veterans. He was also cofounder of the Battle Born Detachment Marine Corps and the Purple Heart 719 First Chapter of Reno. His proudest accomplishment was to create a memorial to honor the Americans Forgotten Korean Casualties in Section U marked "Korean-Unknown" at the National Cemetery of the Pacific (Punchbowl) in Honolulu.

After Bob passed on, his wife gave me all of Bob's poems, she said to please see that the public would get to see all of his poems. I said someday I will write a book about Bob and his poems and that I have your permission to publicize them so others in the future can read about the Korean War.

CHAPTER 21

HONOR FLIGHT NEVADA

It was over ten years ago that I met a young fellow named Jon Yuspa, who worked for Southwest Airlines, and he had transferred to Reno from Baltimore Maryland. Somehow, he got my number and called me to introduce himself and said that he had just arrived in Reno and he wanted to meet people. I suggested to him to come and join the Marine Corps League so that he could meet the people at our meetings. Jon said that he was not a veteran, and I told him not to worry, I would introduce him to the group and sponsor him as an "associate, ember." This started a friendship that has lasted for a long time.

One day Jon asked me if I knew anyone who had a nonprofit corporation that might want to sell. I asked Jon why he wanted a nonprofit, and he told me that when he was in Baltimore, there was a group called "Honor Flight." He said that they fly veterans to Washington, DC, and they pay all the expenses for the veterans to visit the war memorials there. They house and feed them with no expense at all to the veterans.

I told Jon that it was a great idea because Reno and the surrounding cities have a large number of WWII, Korean, and Vietnam veterans that would love to join. I asked him to look into what it would take to form a nonprofit corporation here in Nevada. A few weeks later, Jon called and asked to meet me for breakfast because he had two gentlemen for me to meet. One was a retired gunnery sergeant and the other was Bill, a veteran from Fernley.

Well, we met for breakfast, and I met the two gentlemen and Jon discussed what he had in mind about forming this nonprofit. I told Jon I would be the financial officer, and the Gunny and Bill said that they would do all the legwork to get veterans to join our group. This was how it all began.

Gunny and Bill really worked their butts off, making phone calls and even going to the homes of the veterans in Fernley. One day at a meeting, Jon said that we have enough veterans for our first flight, and we are ready to go. He told me that everything was set with the main Honor Flight office, and that we have our corporation and federal ID number, so let's go. And we'll be known as Honor Flight Nevada.

I asked Jon what were we going to do for money to purchase tickets, hotel rooms, food, and transportation to get the veterans to Washington, DC. "Don't worry," he told me. He would put all the expenses on his credit card. But I also wondered what about when we get back in town, how would we pay off the credit cards? Jon was optimistic and told me not to worry again because he knew the money would come in after the public heard about what we were doing. Jon was right, and after I spent a few sleepless nights, our first trip was a huge success, and the public responded with amazing donations.

After a few more trips with veterans from WWII and Korea, Jon asked me if I had any contacts in Las Vegas, and I told him about a member of the Military Order of the Purple Heart in Las Vegas that I knew. Since we were having great success in northern Nevada, Jon thought to invite southern Nevada to join our group so that more veterans from the state could share in our success.

Jon flew to Las Vegas and met with my friend and a few other gentlemen interested in this, and Jon told them about our process. He showed them how to organize the trips, how to organize the public relations, and how to connect with the veterans. This was great, because they found veterans for their first flight and had a great time in Washington, DC, and returned home. This was broadcast to all of Clark County. When Jon called them to congratulate them on their first success, they told him, "Thanks for all the help, and now we don't need you." They are known as Honor Flight of Southern Nevada, but we are still known as Honor Flight Nevada. I really couldn't believe that my so-called friend had pulled this on us. So much for friends!

We have had great success, especially with forming a single trip with just Vietnam veterans, and then another trip with all Native American veterans. But now a sad thing is happening, and that is our World War II veterans list is getting shorter every day. It seems that they enjoy going and seeing their World War II Memorial, and after they get back home, the trip was at the top of their bucket list to complete.

CHAPTER 22

KAUAI, HAWAII

It was in 1967 that our son started to hang out with some rough kids, and I wanted to place him into a military school, but my wife would not go along with it. My older brother had a son, Terry, that lived in Kauai, Hawaii, at the time. I remembered that when we were in Hawaii, we had visited Kauai and found it to be like the old Hawaii, and not very crowded. So Anne, Ken Junior, and I set off to visit Kauai and Terry to find Ken Junior a new place to live. When we arrived, we checked in to a hotel and then went to see Terry, and he showed us the true Hawaii. Then I finally realized why he was living here. He took us to a shopping center called the Coconut Plantation, and I told Terry that I thought what they needed was a Levi's store. He thought that was a great idea. Over dinner, I asked Terry what he thought about me opening a Levi's store, and if he would run it and hire the people to work in the store. I asked him if maybe Ken Junior could stay there so that he could finish his last year of high school, and we would pay his expenses to stay with Terry and his family. We asked Ken Junior if he would like that, and it was like asking him if he would like some more ice cream. It was a yes, and so Terry, Anne, and I laid out our plans. We decided to return to the mainland so that I could begin to make contacts for our new venture.

When we got back home, I contacted the Levi's corporate office, stated my plans, and they thought it was a great idea since it would be the first Levi's store in Kauai. I then contacted the managers at the

Coconut Plantation shopping center and asked if they had a vacant space in their shopping center, and then I found out who to contact for a lease on the space. They made arrangements with the managers in Honolulu and made an appointment for us to meet. So I got my plane tickets and called Terry to pick me up at six o'clock the next night so we could get started.

When I arrived in Kauai, I contacted a carpenter to have him get our store ready for a grand opening. I found out that things don't move very fast on Kauai, and I had a very hard time ordering supplies. It turned out that I had to include an extra few hundred dollars to motivate them to expedite my orders. Once I found this out, things moved along at a faster pace. While the store was being finished, I again contacted Levi's and started to place my order.

While all this was taking place, I called Anne and asked her to come out, and we would look for a place to live. Anne arrived, and we enrolled Ken Junior at Kapaau High School and met his teacher and the other new students. You should have seen the looks on their faces when we introduced our son. Here was this good-looking teen-aged boy with long blonde hair and a smile to melt anyone. The first thing they said was "Hey, brother, welcome." We knew our problems were over with him.

The store was opened, and we named it after Anne's great-grandmother, "Tennessee Levi's," and it was a great success, especially for the locals and all the Japanese tourists. Then Anne and I heard that there was a new condominium project being built not far from the store, and it was on the beach. We checked into it and found the price to be reasonable, so we bought it for $85,000. It would be finished in five weeks and was a third-floor unit with a great view. It had two bedrooms and two baths, with one up and one down, and a very large living room. There was also a lovely lanai (balcony) to sit and enjoy the view. Now everything was set up to our satisfaction, and we could go home.

Anne's mother had retired from her job, and she had just lost her husband, Foster, and she didn't know what she would do in her retirement. We asked her if she would like to live on the island of Kauai, Hawaii, where she could run our Levi's store and have her grandson there to visit with. It didn't take her long to decide, and she said yes. This was great, but we had a problem because we knew that she would not live with my nephew Terry. We had to find her a place to live, so we all took a trip to Kauai to look around, and she liked a place in Lihue that was right on the Nawiliwili Harbor. It was a two-bedroom condo that we purchased and then returned home so she could pack up everything and move. Three weeks later, she was in her new home on Kauai with a new job and everyone was happy, problem solved.

Things were moving along well for Ken Junior. He was having a good time in school and making new friends. They taught him how to surf better, and he was working in the Levi's store when he was out of school. Granny, my mother-in-law, enjoyed working in the store. The weather was beautiful and warm with tropical breezes in the evening. Life was great. Ken would bring his friends to our condo, but I could not understand them when they spoke. I asked Ken, "What language are they speaking?" He laughed and said that it was called pigeon, which is a form of Hawaiian language that the bishop taught them when they came to the island.

At my business in Glendale, the jobs were running smoothly, and I was involved in a fourteen-story building project that allowed me to spend more time on Kauai. While we were on the island, Anne wanted some tilework and other things done, so I hired a Japanese American contractor to do the work. We hit it off nicely and became good friends later. When the job was done, we went out to celebrate with him and his Japanese wife, and Anne and I had a great time, but it was time to go home.

About three months later, Anne's mother was having a problem with the place where she was living. It seemed that they were doing construction and making a lot of noise, and she couldn't sleep. She then found a nice brand-new three-bedroom home on a large lot, so I told her to sell her condo and buy the house. She had no problem selling her condo and soon she was moving into her new home. Once again, after making all the arrangements and helping her make the move, we returned home very tired.

It was now 1980, and we were very busy, and things were moving pretty fast. We moved to Reno in 1977, and after we got settled,

I decided it was time to start a new adventure when my wife told me I was getting on her nerves. That was when I started Nev-Tex Oil and Gas, Inc. and grew it into an operation that was drilling and producing five wells. I also built a gas transmission business to move and sell my gas. Later I started selling gas to other producers. The Levi's store business was doing fine, Ken was about ready to graduate, and Granny was having a good time. She hired a man to dig up half of her yard so that she could plant a garden. Suzanne was getting used to Reno and making friends at school, and even my dog was happy.

In 1981, Anne and I went on a cruise for a week and spent some time in Pennsylvania with my cousin and his wife and then we returned home. It seemed that Anne was very tired because she loved to take a very hot bath, jump in to bed, and then read until she fell asleep. On July 18, after a great meal, she decided to take her hot bath and jumped in bed to read her book until she fell asleep. And then my son, who was at home visiting, came into the room and told me that he didn't like the color on her face. I jumped up, had someone call an ambulance, and then I ran to get Dr. Bruce. He was with her when the ambulance arrived and transported her to the hospital. I was sitting in the waiting room when the doctor came out and informed me that she had died. My children came in and hugged me, and we all started to cry.

It was never the same after Anne died because I lost interest in everything. Everything in Hawaii and in all my business ventures. I discovered that you really find out who your friends are when you have a tragedy.

CHAPTER 23

NORTHERN NEVADA
TOYS FOR TOTS

It was now 2011. The Forth Force Battalion was stationed in Stead, Nevada, and they got the word that they were being disbanded, and so they had to find someone to take over the Toys for Tots program. They called the Battle Born Detachment to ask if we would be interested. I discussed this at our meeting, but there were no takers, no one was interested. I informed the Marines and said that I had no takers for this project, and they said, "What about you?" I thought about it for a minute and asked them what would be involved and how much time it would take out of my schedule. They said that it was a piece of cake. You would make out a few reports, collect toys, and give them out to needy children. And besides, they would help out if needed. I thought about it, and if they were being transferred to Hawaii, how in the name of hell were they going to help? They said they were as close as your computer. I asked what to do and who to contact. They told me that I just needed to contact the Toys for Tots Foundation, and they would send me some paperwork to complete, and they would let me know.

Within a few days, they contacted me and said they were sending me some paperwork and information for the people to contact, and they would get back to me. I filled out all that was required, called the people, and waited. One week later, I received an email that told me that I was accepted and "Welcome aboard." I called the sergeant who ran Toys for Tots and told him I was now the new coordinator for Toys for Tots in Reno, now what the hell it is that I'm supposed to do? "Well, first off," he said, "you can take over our lease on the storage shed, and then you better call these people about where to put boxes for the public to deposit toys. Tell you what, let's meet at the storage shed and we can talk." Okay, where the hell is this place, and he told me and said we will meet you there in fifteen minutes. They arrived, unlocked the shed, and said, "This is where we keep our overflow of toys." It was empty except for a pallet jack, a desk, and one chair. I was now alone and had to move fast. This was the first of September, and the drive would start on October 1. I called the foundation and made arrangements for me to attend an orientation to get acquainted with my new job. I traveled to Virginia and met my new account manager who seemed like a nice person. I attended a lesson and jotted down notes on what to do and what not to do. This lasted only three days, and it was over that fast. Now it was time to go home. First thing on the agenda was to ask the sergeant who to contact for a building to collect and store the toys. He gave me their phone number, so I called, and he asked if I had a truck. "No, I didn't have a truck." Okay, they gave me a number to call and said, "Talk to Kyle." So I called Kyle at Champion Chevrolet and introduced myself. He said to come over and let's talk. I rushed over there and met Kyle, and then told him my plans for what I was going to do. Then he asked me if I wanted a pickup or a van, and I said a pickup would be easier to work out of. He said, "Good, let's go get one." This started what would turn out to be a friendship for a very long time.

It was now October 1, and the foundation had given me a budget of $20,000 to spend on toys plus a list of toy suppliers. I called the number for a building, and they said they had a vacant old warehouse that I could use. "If you could meet with someone, we can look it over together." We met and walked through. The building had an office, a good-working bathroom, and a pull-up receiving door. This building was twelve thousand square feet, and I thought that I would never use all that space. They agreed to clean it up and remove the trash, on the one condition that we kept the thermostat at sixty-nine degrees, so the pipes wouldn't freeze and burst. I agreed.

I was ready to start on this new venture. I had a volunteer from the Marine Corps League, I had money, and I had a building and a truck. What else did I need? Well, the $20,000 didn't last long, so I called the foundation and said I need more money. They told me to go ahead and place your orders, and we will approve them. I did that and spent another $10,000. The toy shipment started to arrive. I had Don call schools and nonprofit groups and tell them that I was the new coordinator, and I had lots of toys to give away. Things were beginning to happen, and soon I got more volunteers, and we started to collect and give out toys. Our building was working fine, and all the space was getting full. It was now December 15, and we were ready to close our project for the year. We had thirty-five thousand toys collected and given out with no leftover inventory. Not too bad for a first year.

Over the next eight years, we worked out of buildings that had no heat or air conditioning. They were dirty, drafty, cold, and with mice and more. We worked over ten or twelve hours a day, seven days a week, without lunch or dinner, but absolutely loving it. It was worth seeing the expressions on the children's faces, thanking the news media and the many people who donated toys and money. It was very heartwarming.

It is now 2020, and what turned out to be the ninth and last year of my being Northern Nevada coordinator for Toys for Tots. Since I had taken over the organization, my girls and I had established an appointment system to interview, qualify, and organize the process to give toys to their families. Everything was running smoothly until a twosome came along that had other ideas. They wanted to have a civilian take over Toys for Tots and have it run with branches of other local military groups. I objected because this is a Marine organization and should stay with the Marines. Well, politics entered the mix, and it happens that these two people were some of the worst candy-ass Marine officers and hypocrites I have ever seen. I have no idea how they got into the Marine Corps; in fact, they never would have made it with Chesty Puller because he would have fired them on the spot. Nevertheless, I was told by the foundation to step down. I would have liked to finish my tenth year as coordinator and hit the milestone of 1 million toys collected and given out, but it wasn't to be. I am very proud that over 879,000 toys were received, bought, or given out to our needy families and children in northern Nevada. This exceeded the other two county's Toys for Tots coordinators every year. And I'm also proud that we came a long way for our kids because I am a firm believer that "Every child shall have a happy Christmas."

Semper fi.

CHAPTER 24

SECTION U

The year was 1991, and the "Chosin Few" were having their National Convention in Honolulu, Hawaii. Our group from Reno, Nevada, consisted of ten Marines. We decided to attend since the Veterans Administration had their agency head attending, and there were several medical questions that we were going to discuss.

While we were there, we traveled to the Punchbowl National Cemetery to fill in our time. We checked in with the Marine colonel who oversaw the Punchbowl, and he asked if we were interested in seeing Section U. He informed us that this was the section that was set aside for veterans that fought in Korea. We approached this section, and we saw that there were 825 graves with the inscription on their headstones that read "Korea Unknown." We were taken aback because we had no idea that there so many from Korea that had no names for the veterans, or where they were killed.

When we returned to our hotel, we had a meeting and talked about what we had just seen. One of our group members said, "Those poor bastards had no identity, and no one seems to care about it or give a shit." Bob Holtzer, who was known for writing poems, stayed up all night composing a poem on what he had seen that day.

The next morning at breakfast, Bob read the poem he had written and wanted our input on it. We told Bob that it was one of the best poems he had ever written. Then we went on to talk about what we can do with it. It was suggested that we have a slab of granite that

THE TOOTSIE ROLL MARINES

was gray in color, and we would have Bob's poem inscribed on it as a tribute to those that were laid to rest in Section U. We all agreed that this was a great idea, and we decided that we would ship it to Honolulu, Hawaii, and make arrangements with the Marine colonel at Punchbowl to get permission to present it in memory of the "unknown." We told the colonel that this was our donation from the Nevada group, and it would have nothing to do with the National Chosin Few.

When the stone was ready with the poem inscribed, each of us dug into our pockets and came up with the money to ship it to the Punchbowl in Hawaii. "Okay, guys, now what?" We decided to set a date to travel to the Punchbowl and present it to the cemetery. So we made our reservations with the airlines and hotels in Hawaii, and everything was set and off we went on a very special journey.

While at the Chosin Few convention, we made connections with another Korean veteran who lived in Honolulu, Hawaii. He was in the Air Force and his name was David Moffat. We became good friends with David, and we told him what we were planning to do. He was very excited and said he had noticed that there was nothing about this in the local papers or any media about the Punchbowl Section U. David then invited Bob Holtzer, Darrel Deal, an army veteran who served in Korea who had always wanted to be a Marine, and myself to his home for dinner and to meet his wife and his son. She was born in Japan and had a special affinity for American veterans. His son, David Junior, was there too. We talked about the cemetery and the monument that we were going to ship, and we also discussed that we would like to have a flower arrangement placed at Section U every Memorial Day. David said that he would be more than happy to place the flowers every year. This was great; so every year, we sent money to David for the flowers.

Seven years later, we received a phone call from David Junior that his dad passed on and that he would be proud to take his dad's place and continue to arrange for the flowers to be at Section U every year.

Fast forward to December 2021, when I was in Hawaii with Honor Flight Nevada for the Pearl Harbor eightieth-year ceremony, and I arranged to meet with David and his family. His Japanese mother was also there. Boy, I was shocked, because the last time we met, David Junior was just twelve years old. I realized that this was over thirty years ago, and this little kid was now six-foot-three-inch tall and married with two children of his own. David's mother-in-law was half-Japanese and half-Korean, and it turns out she was a little girl when I was in Korea. When I talked about our battle of the downtown train station, she remembered this and told her daughter about it. She said that if the Marines were not there to fight the North Koreans that she and her daughter would not be there today.

These days I've realized that almost all my Marine buddies have passed on, and it seems that I'm the last one still around, so it's important to me to be close with David and his family. When we were on a trip with Honor Flight Nevada last year, we got to view our memorial at the Punchbowl. I was honored to explain how we got involved in placing flowers on the graves every Memorial Day for over thirty-five years, and how the American public had never been told about these brave veterans in Section U. They fought for our country and never received any recognition for it, and somehow there was something very wrong with this picture, however, they will always have their memorial.

The article below is from May 16, 2023, and details the ongoing efforts to disinter those in Section U.

Defense POW/MIA Accounting Agency—
Fulfilling Our Nation's Promise

Disinterring Korean War Unknowns

In 2019, the Defense POW/MIA Accounting Agency began disinterring 652 sets of unknown remains associated with the Korean War that had been buried at the National Memorial Cemetery of the Pacific (NMCP), better known as the Punchbowl. The unknown remains in question were recovered from the

Republic of Korea (ROK, South Korea) and Democratic Republic of Korea (DPRK, North Korea) in the 1950s and 1960s, and were buried as unknowns after they could not be identified by the traditional forensic processes available at the time.

Given the large number of remains, the plan is to disinter the remains in seven phases over the next five to seven years. The phases are based on the geographic region where the remains were recovered and other criteria that provides sequential logic to this complex identification process. Conducting the disinterment in this manner is more efficient and effective as it allows researchers and scientists to focus on sets of individuals with similar history and circumstances of loss. As the remains are identified in this method, it will reduce the potential candidates for subsequent phases, and thereby provide quicker identifications.

Each of the seven phases will include unknowns recovered from North and South Korea. The phases are also balanced between sets of remains that are more complete, those that are made up of fewer remains, remains that are not well preserved, or those that have been commingled with other unknowns. The latter group will require more time and resources to identify. DPAA will work with the Armed Forces Medical Examiner System-Armed Forces DNA Identification Laboratory (AFMES-AFDIL) to identify the remains, and NMCP will further refine the exhumation schedule within each phase to balance cases that need additional resources or scheduling due to capacity or logistical considerations.

As a result of this effort, the Department will no longer divert resources to trying to work and address individual requests on a by-case basis, a process that had proven both inefficient and frustrating for families, because the remains more often than not turned out to be someone other than their loved one. However, as each unknown is analyzed for identification, all Family Reference Sample (FRS) data on file will be compared against the unknown DNA sample, therefore providing identification of individuals who may have been thought to be in later phases.

Based on the results of this effort, DPAA will consider this plan for future large-scale disinterment projects.

(https://dpaa-mil.sites.crmforce.mil/dpaaFam WebKoreanWar Disinternments)

CHAPTER 25

A BRIEF ACCOUNT OF
THE KOREAN WAR

The clever and risky operation of landing at Incheon far behind enemy lines was conceived by General Douglas MacArthur on his personal reconnaissance trip to Korea, June 29, but it had to be postponed for him to commit the Marines he planned to use to delay the North Korean steamroller pushing down the peninsula.

The navy and Marines, the countries experts, as well as most army people not on MacArthur's staff, were against the operation. One admiral said, "We drew up a list of every natural and geographic possibility for an amphibious landing and Incheon had them all." The narrow channel at the landing site could easily be blocked when currents were at eight knots. There were no beaches, and only the easily defended city of Incheon and many more were close by. The worst of all were the thirty-three feet high tides, which left nothing but mud flats at low tide. After sixty-five minutes of a gloomy presentation of the obstacles, it was concluded that while it would be a most difficult operation, it was not impossible. Present at this meeting were the chiefs of the navy, the army, the Fifth Air Force, and General MacArthur and some of his staff.

MacArthur then made a masterful presentation of the complex military operation. "Spellbinding" was how Navy Chief Admiral Forrest Sherman and Army Chief General J. Lawton Collins described it. Admiral James Doyle said that if MacArthur had gone on stage, he would have been compared to John Barrymore, the famous American actor of the 1920s and 1930s.

The Incheon Landing became one of the most brilliant moves in American history. The slaughter, which consisted of the armies slugging it out head-to-head and toe-to-toe around the Pusan perimeter, would cease, thousands of casualties would be prevented, and a decisive victory would be won.

No other nation in the world had the means and the knowledge to put together over two hundred ships to land seventy thousand troops successfully in such a precarious place on such short notice. "The navy has never shone more brightly" were the words of the Far East commander who said, "Give me my Marines, and they will do it."

The First Marine Division landed a battalion on Wolmi-Do, the fortified island guarding the entrance to Incheon at 6:33 a.m. on September 15, 1950. An hour later, the island was secure. Because of the high tides, the next twelve hours would be sweated out before other landings at Incheon proper could take place. When they did land, the First Marine Regiment and the remainder of the fifth reached their objectives with light opposition from the surprised enemy; Marine and naval air ruled the skies.

The Republic of Korea (ROK) Marines occupied Incheon while the Marines moved out to personnel fleeing from the south and linked up with forces breaking toward Seoul twenty miles away. The Seventh US Army Infantry Division landed south of the city to protect the Marines flank, cutting off the North Korean People's Army (NKPA) personnel fleeing from the south and linking up with forces breaking out of the Pusan perimeter.

The landing troops were designated X Corps and under the command of Major General Almond, a brusque, overbearing officer who had offended the First Marine Division commander, General Oliver P. Smith, who was resentful of being under army command. As the Marines attacked the heavily fortified area west of Seoul, General Smith refused, saying that he wanted to keep his regiments together. As Marine casualties continue to mount, Almond sent the army's Thirty-Second Regiment across without losing a man or a piece of equipment. They were followed by the Seventeenth ROK regiment. After a strong attack on the army unit, the major NKPA force withdrew, but their rear guard continued to offer stiff resistance to the Marines, who were fighting block by block into the heart of the city.

CHAPTER 26

THE CHOSIN RESERVOIR

(An Excerpt from *Encyclopedia Britannica*)

Men and armor of the US First Marine Division during the
Battle of the Chosin Reservoir, North Korea, December 1950.
Photo by Corporal Peter McDonald, US Marine Corps.

Battle of the Chosin Reservoir, or Chosin, also called Changjin,
campaign early in the Korean War, was part of the Chinese Second
Offensive (November–December 1950) to drive the United Nations

out of North Korea. The Chosin Reservoir campaign was directed mainly against the First Marine Division of the US X Corps, which had disembarked in eastern North Korea and moved inland in severe winter weather to a mountainous area near the reservoir. The campaign succeeded in forcing the entire X Corps to evacuate to South Korea, but the Chinese did not achieve their particular objective of isolating and destroying the First Marine Division. Instead, in a deliberate retrograde movement that has become one of the most-storied exploits in Marine Corps lore, the Marines turned and fought their way down a narrow vulnerable road through several mountain passes and a bridged chasm until they reached transport ships waiting at the coast.

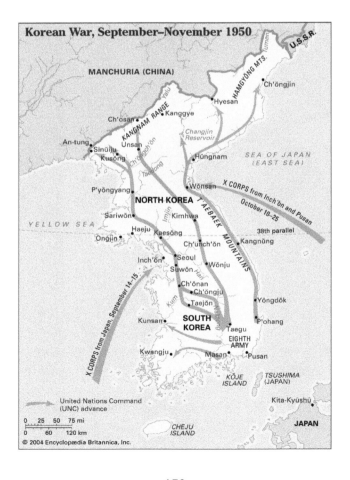

Men of the Seventh Regiment, US First Marine Division, wearing and carrying cold-weather gear, moving toward the Chosin Reservoir, North Korea, on November 1, 1950. US Marine Corps or National Archives and Records Administration.

Crossing into North Korea

Following the successful landing of the X Corps at Incheon in September 1950, the United Nations Command (UNC), under the direction of US President Harry S. Truman's administration and the UN General Assembly, pursued the remnants of the communist Korean People's Army into North Korea. On the orders of General Douglas MacArthur, commander of all allied forces in the UNC, the US Eighth Army crossed the thirty-eighth parallel (the pre-war border) on October 7 and advanced up the western side of the Korean peninsula toward Pyongyang, the capital of the Democratic People's Republic of Korea. At the same time, MacArthur redeployed the X Corps on amphibious ships around the peninsula to Korea's east coast. The X Corps (commanded by Major General Edward M. Almond) included the First Marine Division (Major General Oliver P. ["O. P."] Smith), the Seventh Infantry Division (Major General David G. Barr), and the Third Infantry Division (Major General Robert H. Soule). The corps also had control of the capital and third divisions of the South Korean I Corps, which was already crossing the thirty-eighth parallel on the east-coast highway.

What MacArthur did not know was that the Chinese had feared such an offensive since the Incheon Landing. The Chinese began preparations to enter the war by sending supplies and support troops into North Korea. Meanwhile, Chinese combat divisions, some twenty-one in number but expanding to thirty-three by December, remained in Manchuria ready to move against the UNC ground forces. On October 18–19, Chinese leader Mao Zedong, after considerable debate, ordered the Chinese People's Volunteers Force (CPVF), under the command of General Peng Dehuai, to move against the Eighth Army, whose lead elements had advanced beyond Pyongyang and were marching along two separate routes toward the border with China at the Yalu River. The Chinese First Offensive of October 25 to November 6 staggered the Eighth Army, damaging one American division and four South Korean divisions in the battle of Onjŏng-Unsan. To the east, two American divisions of the X Corps had landed on October 26 and 29, and the South Korean I Corps was heading north up the coast road toward the Sino-Soviet border. The wide separation of these units made them a tempting objective for the Chinese. On November 2–4, the South Koreans and US Marines fought their first engagement against the Chinese at Sudong, inland from the port city of Hŭngnam. There a Marine regiment defeated an attacking division, killing at least 662 Chinese soldiers.

Men of the Seventh Regiment, US First Marine Division,
during the advance toward the Chosin Reservoir, North Korea,
early November 1950. US Department of Defense.

Advancing to Chosin

Underestimating the fighting ability of the CPVF, MacArthur ordered Almond to advance inland with the First Marine and Seventh Infantry divisions to the Chosin Reservoir. From there the two divisions would move west toward Kanggye, a mountain mining town where the Chinese and North Korean armies seemed to be concentrating—a maneuver that would place the X Corps north of and behind the CPVF armies facing the Eighth Army. MacArthur's scheme required an 88-km (55-mile) advance over a single unpaved road through the heart of the Taebaek Mountains in freezing weather and blinding snowstorms. Smith told Almond the plan was rash, but Almond, operating directly under MacArthur, ordered the Marines forward.

A US Marine camp at Hagaru-Ri, North Korea, during
the Battle of the Chosin Reservoir, November–December
1950. Photo by Sergeant Frank C. Kerr, US Marine Corps,
National Archives and Records Administration.

The X Corps' first objective, the village of Hagaru-Ri, rested near
the southern tip of the reservoir, a narrow mountain lake that provided
hydroelectric power to the mining industries of northern Korea. The
lake's proper name is the Changjin Reservoir, but during Japan's annex-
ation of Korea (1910–45), its name had been changed to Chōsen, the
Japanese name for Korea. Through successive translations and hurried
mapmaking, the reservoir became known as Chosin and remains so to
this day for American veterans of the Korean War. By any name, it was
a cold barren battleground where deep foxholes could be dug into the
frozen earth only with the help of explosives and bulldozers.

With its supplies moving by truck, the First Marine Division
established battalion-sized bases at Chinhŭng-Ni and Koto-Ri, villages
along the Main Supply Route (MSR), the X Corps' name for the road
to the reservoir. The division began its final march to the reservoir on
November 13, with two of its reinforced regiments, the Seventh and
Fifth Marines, in column and moving cautiously. Each regiment was a

regimental combat team with attached artillery battalions, a tank company, engineers, and headquarters and service units. On November 15, lead elements of the Seventh Marines reached Hagaru-Ri. From there the regiment prepared for its next advance, west of the reservoir to Yudam-Ni, 22 km (14 miles) away, while the Fifth Marines moved cautiously up the reservoir's right bank. General Smith, unhappy with this risky deployment, persuaded Almond to allow the Marines to concentrate at Hagaru-Ri and replace the eastern force with a unit from the Seventh Infantry Division. Almond ordered General Barr to form a regimental combat team of two infantry battalions, an artillery battalion, and other troops. The Thirty-First Infantry Regiment, commanded by Colonel Allan D. MacLean and known as Task Force MacLean, numbered 3,200 Americans and Koreans. It replaced the Marines east of the reservoir on November 25. Smith used this operational pause to strengthen the defenses of Hagaru-Ri and build a rough airfield for emergency resupply and medical evacuations. A battalion of Marines manned the most vulnerable part of the perimeter, but much of the position had to be manned by noninfantry units. The Marine Corps' investment in making "every Marine a rifleman" would soon pay dividends.

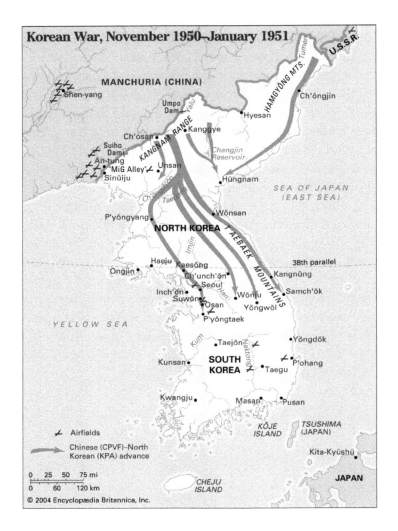

Korean War, November 1950–January 1951

The Chinese Strike

As the First Marine Division advanced, Peng ordered the uncommitted Ninth Army Group (commanded by General Song Shilun) to leave Manchuria and destroy it. Song's army group (twelve divisions in three armies) numbered 150,000 soldiers—mostly infantry with mortars and machine guns but not much artillery, since the Chinese lacked guns, shells, and trucks and feared UNC air strikes on road-bound columns. Moreover, the army group had not prepared for winter war. Still, Mao found the X Corps too tempting a target to resist, and the Chinese believed they had found an effective formula for fighting the UNC—stealth, nighttime attacks, ambushes, local surprise, and superiority in numbers. The Ninth Army Group moved into positions on either side of the reservoir with five divisions, and it moved three more divisions to cut the road south of Hagaru-Ri and attack Koto-Ri. Smith, benefiting from aggressive intelligence operations, knew the Chinese had massed around his division, but Almond did not share his alarm.

In the last week of November the Ninth Army Group launched simultaneous division-level attacks on the First Marine Division at Yudam-Ni, Hagaru-Ri, and Koto-Ri and on Task Force MacLean east of the reservoir. The Seventh and Fifth Marines, having met major Chinese forces in a daylight attack on November 27, quickly prepared a perimeter defense for night action. The enclaves at Hagaru-Ri and Koto-Ri were even better prepared, though the Hagaru-Ri perimeter had too much critical hill terrain to defend with the available troops. Halfway between Yudam-Ni and Hagaru-Ri, one Marine rifle company defended Tŏktong Pass, where the Chinese Fifty-Ninth Division had placed a major roadblock. Task Force MacLean, meanwhile, was strung out along the east shoreline road in seven different locations. In three days of intense night battles and daylight probes starting on the night of November 27–28, all the major Marine positions held, but Task Force MacLean did not. By the time the surviving soldiers (minus their commanding officer, who went missing in action enroute and was never recovered) managed to struggle on foot and in small, disorganized groups around the frozen reservoir or directly across the ice to Hagaru-Ri, they numbered only 670, and only half of them were fit for duty. The Marine regiments, on the other hand, though reduced by one-third to one-half in their rifle companies, managed to halt or curb the Chinese attacks, aimed at penetrating the perimeters and overrunning artillery positions, the airfield, and command posts. Artillery fire around the clock and air strikes during the day also punished the Chinese. The only real misstep in the defensive battle was a decision by Smith and the First Marine Regiment commander,

Colonel Lewis B. ("Chesty") Puller, to send a convoy of tanks and supply trucks from Koto-Ri to Hagaru-Ri on November 29. Task Force
Drysdale, commanded by Lieutenant Colonel Douglas B. Drysdale,
Forty-One Independent Commando, Royal Marines, in addition to
service and headquarters troops, included a Marine infantry company,
an army infantry company, and Drysdale's British raiding battalion.
The task force was ambushed en route. One-third of the force (tanks
and infantry) fought through to Hagaru-Ri, and another third fought
its way back to Koto-Ri. The remainder (162 officers and men) died
or became captives.

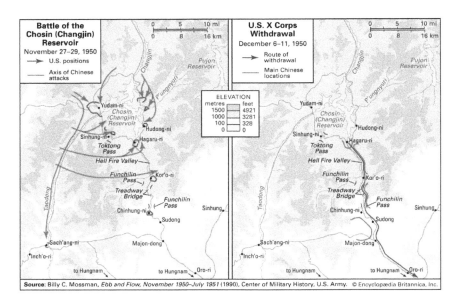

Source: Billy C. Mossman, *Ebb and Flow, November 1950–July 1951* (1990), Center of Military History, U.S. Army. © Encyclopædia Britannica, Inc.

Fighting Back to the Coast

On November 29, Almond, having met with MacArthur in
Tokyo, acknowledged that the X Corps could survive only if its
dispersed divisions headed for the nearest port. Most headed to
Hŭngnam and were evacuated to Wŏnsan—a decision that reflected
the Eighth Army's defeats in the west.

Men of the Fifth and Seventh regiments, US First Marine
Division, receiving an order to withdraw from their positions
near the Chosin Reservoir, North Korea, November 29, 1950.
Photo by Sergeant Frank C. Kerr, US Marine Corps.

Moreover, the Truman administration soon discarded the policy of unifying Korea by force, though it still wanted to save the
Republic of Korea. Preserving the UNC for this mission (its original
one) dictated that the X Corps escape the grasp of the CPVF Ninth
Army Group. To achieve this aim, Almond took a worst-case position: the Yudam-Ni and Hagaru-Ri garrisons would rally at the latter
perimeter and then fly out, abandoning the division's heavy weapons, vehicles, and supplies. The rest of the division would march
back down the MSR from Koto-Ri to Hŭngnam. Smith, however,
refused to abandon his division's equipment. Instead, he argued that
the Yudam-Ni–Hagaru-Ri movement was a critical one. Once the
two groups had united at Hagaru-Ri, they could absorb ammunition
and replacements by air and evacuate the worst wounded and frozen

casualties. At that point the division could turn and fight its way to the coastal plain "advancing in a different direction," as Smith phrased it. Almond conceded that such a withdrawal by the First Marine Division would attract Chinese divisions and thus allow the rest of the X Corps to retreat without real danger.

US Marines unloading a transport plane at Hagaru-Ri, North Korea, during the Battle of the Chosin Reservoir, December 5, 1950. Photo by Corporal McDonald, US Marine Corps, National Archives and Records Administration.

On December 1, the First Marine Division began the movement that eventually took its rear guard inside the perimeter established by the Third Infantry Division near Hŭngnam. In the course of this escape, the division rendered three more Chinese divisions ineffective in addition to the four that had already been ruined at Yudam-Ni and Hagaru-Ri. The Yudam-Ni group, the first to move out, did not stop until it reached Hagaru-Ri on December 4. The Fifth Marines walked the road to protect the vehicle train, while the

Seventh Marines plodded through the hills to break up Chinese "fire sacks" and relieve the Tŏktong Pass defenders. Their two artillery battalions, meanwhile, moved by bounds to ensure continuous fire support, and Marine and navy fighter-bombers were on call during daylight to strike any suspected ambush. The arrival of the Fifth and Seventh Marines at Hagaru-Ri ensured that the airfield would not be closed by Chinese fire. Marine and air force transports brought in critical ammunition and gasoline and took out 4,500 casualties. The fuel was critical: one Marine artillery battalion lost half its guns north of Hagaru-Ri when its tractors ran out of diesel fuel.

Elements of US First Marine Division marching along the main supply route south of Hagaru-Ri, North Korea, during the Battle of the Chosin Reservoir, December 6, 1950. Photo by Sergeant Frank C. Kerr, US Marine Corps, National Archives and Records Administration.

Chinese soldiers taken prisoner by the US Seventh Marine Regiment south of Koto-Ri, North Korea, during the Battle of the Chosin Reservoir, December 9, 1950. Photo by Sergeant Frank C. Kerr, US Marine Corps, National Archives and Records Administration.

The reassembled First Marine Division reorganized, tried to eat, and sleep in warming tents, and prepared to fight south to the coast. On December 6, the "attack in a different direction" continued, destination Koto-Ri, 18 km (11 miles) distant. The real challenge was Funchilin Pass below Koto-Ri, where the Chinese had destroyed a bridge over a chasm. The solution was to assemble a bridge that was air-dropped in sections, enough of which survived to allow vehicles to pass. The Chinese contested the withdrawal at this chokepoint, but the Marines fought through the trap, although the rear guard had to abandon seven tanks. The final potential barrier, another pass to the south, had been cleared by the First Battalion, First Marines, in a nighttime attack in temperatures as low as negative thirty-four degrees Celsius (negative thirty degrees Fahrenheit).

A battalion of the Third Infantry Division stopped two attacks on the final Hŭngnam perimeter on December 3 and 15. By the latter date the First Marine Division, its rear guard having reached Hŭngnam on December 11, had been loaded onto their waiting transport ships. Resistance by the Chinese had become almost token, their troops ruined by cold, starvation, and relentless X Corps firepower. The Chosin Reservoir campaign was a geographic victory for the Chinese, for the X Corps, instead of redeploying to Wŏnsan, was forced to return to South Korea, where it became part of the Eighth Army in January 1951. Nevertheless, the campaign ruined the CPVF Ninth Army Group, which did not return to the front until March 1951, and it convinced the UNC that allied ground troops could defeat Chinese armies, however numerous.

Supplies and equipment being loaded onto ships at Hŭngnam, North Korea, after the US retreat from the Chosin Reservoir, December 11, 1950. Photo by Private First Class Emerich M. Christ, US Army, National Archives and Records Administration.

The Chinese have remained vague on their losses in the battle, but their own records and UNC estimates put the Ninth Army Group's casualties in the range of 40,000 to 80,000, when one counts combat deaths and wounded plus deaths and incapacity from the cold. The First Marine Division lost 4,385 men to combat and 7,338 to the cold. Other X Corps losses amounted to some 6,000 Americans and Koreans.

CHAPTER 27

NORTH KOREA INCURSION

The Incheon Landing had changed the fortunes of war almost overnight, insuring a NKPA defeat. General Matthew Ridgway said that if it had been suggested that MacArthur could walk on water, most would have believed it. But now the far east commander made a serious mistake.

On September 27, he was ordered by the joint chief of staff to cross the thirty-eighth parallel without fanfare and with little publicity. The objective was to destroy the remaining NKPA forces and unite the North under the Government of South Korea. With some reluctance, the United Nations approved this action. Some of the reasons given were: 1) 2,599 American and 25,000 ROK POWs were being held; 2) Red China, which had massive economic and social problems and an army lacking armor, heavy artillery, and air support, would probably not intervene; 3) taking North Korea away from Russian influence would increase US chances of rapprochement with China; 4) if left intact, North Korea might invade again after it recovered; 5) Syngman Rhee was intent on unifying the country and would be difficult to hold in check; 6) Americans were outraged at the atrocities committed by the enemy against US forces; and 7) with the total victory of World War II so recent, it would be hard for the Truman administration, accused of being soft on Communism, to settle for anything less.

MacArthur was to engage any Chinese forces encountered in Korea as long as, in his judgment, action by forces now under his control offered a good chance of success.

Fearing stubborn resistance at the North Korean capital of Pyongyang, MacArthur withdrew the X Corps and landed it on the east coast so that it would attack across the "narrow waist" of Korea, toward Pyongyang from the east, while the Eighth Army attacked from the south. This was a tragic mistake, not only because of the delay it caused, which allowed some recovery among NKPA units and time for the Chinese to deploy unseen in Korea, but it over-loaded the transportation system that was heavily damaged by UN bombing—to the extent that it was very difficult to keep the Eighth Army supplied for its incursion into North Korea. It so happened that resistance was light, and Pyongyang was taken by the First CAV and First ROK Division on October 19. The ROK troops advanced so rapidly up the east coast that they took the landing site of Wonsan before the X Corps arrived by sea.

A perfectly executed air drop by the 187th Airborne Regimental Combat Team north of Pyongyang was too late to rescue a trainload of US POWs, who were massacred before the paratroopers landed. A NKPA force of 500 was caught between the 187th and the Australian Battalion, and the 27th British Commonwealth Brigade were advancing to link up with their troopers. Fearing their fire would hit the Americans, they fixed bayonets and charged the enemy, killing 270 and capturing 200, while miraculously sustaining only seven wounded of their own.

CHAPTER 28

CHINESE INTERVENTION

By the 1860s, expansionist Russia, under the Czars, reached the Pacific under the leadership of Vladivostok. Defeated in a conflict with Japan (1904–1906), Russia had regarded that country as her natural enemy in the area. During the 1930's and during World War II, Joseph Stalin had supported the Nationalist Chinese under Chang Kai-Shek because, from a practical standpoint, they were the only force capable of opposing the Japanese at that time.

Popular with the Chinese Communists was Mao Zedong, who although not trained in Moscow as were other Chinese, would become the leader of the party in China. He was in a constant struggle to maintain his leadership and to avoid destruction from his sworn enemy Chiang Kai-Shek. Relations between Mao and Stalin were cool.

When the Nationalists were defeated in October 1949 and the People's Republic of China was established by the communists, US far eastern policy changed. Support for Chiang had ceased sometime before because his corrupt regime did not have popular support.

In December of 1949, US embassies were advised that should Formosa (Taiwan)—where the Nationalists had fled—fall to the Communists, it was not to be considered a threat to US security. A rapprochement would be made to the People's Republic, showing that Russia, coveting Manchuria as she did, was China's real enemy.

It appears that Stalin became aware of this change. McLean Burgess, and Kim Philby, working in British Intelligence with access to US information, were later discovered to be Soviet spies. (During the war, MacArthur would sense that someone was reading his messages.) Continued success by Mao would make him a rival for the leadership on international communism. As Stalin had promised to help the North Koreans, he had also offered aid to the Chinese who had massed two hundred thousand troops opposite Formosa for the invasion. Did Stalin coerce Kim Il Sung to invade first so that he would have an excuse to delay help to the Chinese? Was his support of the Korean invasion an effort to impede US or China rapprochement?

When the Incheon Landing changed the whole course of the war in Korea, Stalin urged the Chinese to intervene, promising them air power. At an October 1 meeting, most Chinese leaders were against intervention, although 80 percent of Chinese heavy industry was in Manchuria and most dependent on electric power generated from North Korea. General Peng Teh-huai, who would command Chinese Communist Forces (CCF) in Korea, said that if the American reached the Yalu River, the border between Korea and Manchuria, they would find an excuse to invade China. Mao felt that China should come to the aid of its neighbor. A decision was made to intervene, which appeared to be based on their own national interest and not Russian pressure.

Moving at night and using excellent camouflage, troops of the CCF Fourth Field Army (200,000) that were already in Manchuria, crossed into Korea while troops of the Third Field Army (120,000) headed north to reinforce. These forces were undetected by UN air reconnaissance which was mostly employed in a strategic role of location of targets and evaluation of bombing.

UN forces continued their advance and on October 25 at Unsan (oon-san), about seventy miles north of Pyongyang, the ROK Fifteenth Regiment was stopped by the Chinese, who had been deployed in the mountains since October 17. The US Eighth Cavalry Regiment was sent to their aid and was badly mauled, losing a whole Battalion. Then the Chinese mysteriously withdrew. The same thing happened in the eastern sector where the Marines were stopped in their advance to the Chosin Reservoir, and then the enemy withdrew.

Prisoners that were sent back to headquarters were confirmed to be Chinese. Intelligence estimated that there were no more than 27,000 (this was later upgraded to 70,000) Chinese in Korea. There were actually 320,000.

The advance of the 6th Army (118,000 strong) resumed on November 24 despite a shortage of supplies, including winter clothing. Some riflemen had as few as 16 rounds of ammunition. On the night of November 25, the CCF struck the ROK Corps on the Army's right flank with a massive attack which disorganized the South Koreans and sent them reeling to the rear. To the left, the US Second and Twenty-Fifth Divisions were also hit with furious assaults, and they were penetrated in some spots, but they were able to restore the situation and hold. The collapse of the ROK exposed the flank of the Second Division and forced the UN forces to withdraw. Two regiments of the Second were almost destroyed at Kuunu-ri, but the rest of the army withdrew in good order, using their mobility to out distance the slower moving CCF, who could maintain an offensive for only a few days.

In the X Corps sector in the east, one regiment of the Seventh Division reached the Yalu, but the Marines were stopped at the Chosin Reservoir. Oliver Smith, sensing more enemy in the area than was being reported, moved more slowly than Ned Almond was urging him. He stockpiled ammunition and supplies along the way. His caution contributed greatly to saving his command. An army task force of two mismatched battalions, artillery, and other supporting units were hurried into position to protect the Marines right flank.

The bulk of the 120,000 CCF in the area hit the Marines and the Army Task Force. Winter had set in with temperatures of twenty-four degrees below zero. Flesh stuck to metal. Weapons and vehicles froze. In their fighting withdrawal, the Marines inflicted horrendous casualties on the enemy while sustaining 4,418 battle casualties and 7,313 nonbattle casualties (mostly weather-related). For the first time in history, flying boxcars (C-119-type aircraft) dropped a treadway bridge which enabled them to get their heavy equipment out over Funchilin Pass, where a bridge had been destroyed. Paratrooper Fred Fishel said a practice drop in Japan had failed. By December 11, the last man reached the safety of the lodgment area of Hungnam, held by the US Third Division. Plagued by the Katusa factor, low ammunition, and the loss of all four senior commanders, the ill-fated army unit Task Force Maclean or Faith held out for five days and four nights to its own destruction. Of its original strength of 2,500, only 385 were fit for duty, but they did protect the Marines' right flank.

The CCF forced the UN out of North Korea, but at a tremendous cost. Sources favorable to the Communist side estimate that the UN inflicted casualties on their adversary at the rate of twenty to one. It was reported that General Peng flew to Mao's headquarters, dragging him out of bed to complain that the troops were exhausted, and their clothing, equipment, and support was totally unsuited for such a campaign.

The X Corps was evacuated by sea with almost one hundred thousand civilians unwilling to live under communism coming out with them. Because of its right flank the Eighth Army retired to a narrow position about forty-five miles south of the Thirty-Eighth parallel where they were joined by the X Corps.

The UN asked for an armistice at the parallel, but the elated Chinese, who had gained world acclaim, refused to seriously consider the proposal. Pouring in more troops, their goal was the expulsion of UN forces in South Korea. General Walker was killed in a jeep accident on December 24. General Matthew Ridgway was given command of the Eighth Army, which was plagued with defeat, disappointment in the present, and low morale. Ridgway, who believed the right plight of the withdrawal had been greatly exaggerated in the press, soon had his troops turn around and began pushing the CCF and the NKPA back into North Korea. Five Star General Omar Bradley, Chairman of the Joint Chiefs of Staff, said that his brilliant, driving, uncompromising leadership turned the tide of battle as no other general in American history.

CHAPTER 29

AMERICAN POLICY

One false concept which hampered American policy throughout the cold war was that all Communists were directly controlled, and every action was directed from Moscow. Although US Russian experts, such as George Kennan, Chip Bolan, and Averell Harriman believed that the Soviet Union was not ready for war and did not want war, Americans were ready to accept that the North Korean invasion might well be the beginning of World War III. Therefore, the US Seventh Fleet was sent to the Formosa Strait to prevent an invasion from the mainland of Nationalist China. This, of course, sent an entirely hostile signal to the People's Republic to whom, in December 1949, the US was seeking rapprochement.

During World War II, victory in Europe was the first goal, while the Pacific was of secondary priority. After the turnaround in Incheon, the Joint Chiefs asked MacArthur how soon he could release a division for the real concern, or two, for Europe. Here's where the real concern was. The Chinese intervention heightened US fears of World War III. It was in reference to widening the war to mainland China that General Bradley said we would be fighting the wrong war at the wrong place at the wrong time. During the fighting in Korea, six US divisions were sent to Europe, while the most US divisions on the line at any one time in Korea was seven. That's right, seven.

Fearing for Europe, President Truman wanted to cool down the war in Korea. The legendary hero of World War II in the Pacific,

171

Douglas MacArthur, wanted to expand the war, believing a victory in Asia would secure peace in Europe. Although warned, he continued to publicly express these big ideas and he was relieved of command in April 1951. A big uproar ensued, but soon died down in the public mind as the war was to do also.

Seoul had been retaken in March as UN forces continued to push northward. A CCF counteroffensive failed in April to recapture the capitol, and in May in east central Korea, their attack became known as the May Massacre because of their heavy losses. When the war broke out the year before and action was taken by the UN. to support South Korea, the Soviets were boycotting the meetings because Red China had not been admitted. In June of 1951 the Soviet delegate to the UN, Jacob Malik who had returned to the US, proposed truce talks. The Chinese had suffered an unbelievable number of casualties, had shot their bolt, and were asked were they ready to talk peace. The Soviets had lost face in the Communist world. The US had come to the aid of its ally, and South Korea and Russia had not. Chinese influence in North Korea increased as Russia's decreased. Mao gained stature as a world leader. Both Great Britain and the US embarked on huge rearmament programs. NATO became a reality under the command of an American general. West Germany moved toward being a sovereign state, with its own military force. American defense spending in Japan—Toyota was almost bankrupt—propelled her toward being an economic superpower. The Soviets had come up short everywhere. There only success, US–China rapprochement was delayed until President Nixon's time, twenty years later.

CHAPTER 30

THE TOOTSIE ROLL MARINES

On November 26, 1950, fifteen thousand men of the First Marine Division, along with elements of two army regimental combat teams and a detachment of British Royal Marines commandos and some South Korean policemen were completely surrounded by well over ten divisions of Chinese troops in rugged mountains near the Chosin Reservoir. Chairman Mao himself had ordered the Marines annihilated, and Chinese General Song-un gave it his best shot, throwing human waves of his 120,000-plus soldiers against the heavily outnumbered allied forces. A massive cold front blew in from Siberia, and with it, the coldest winter in recorded Korean history. For the encircled allies at the Chosin Reservoir, daytime temperatures averaged five degrees below zero, while nights plunged to minus thirty-five and lower.

Jeep batteries froze and split. C rations ran dangerously low, and the cans were frozen solid. Fuel could not be spared to thaw them. If truck engines stopped, their fuel lines froze. Automatic weapons wouldn't cycle. Morphine syringes had to be thawed in a medical corpsman's mouth before they could be injected. Precious bottles of blood plasma froze. Resupply could only come by air, and that was spotty and erratic because of foul weather.

High command virtually wrote the Marines off, believing that their situation was hopeless. Washington braced for imminent news of slaughter and defeat. Retreat was hardly an option, not

173

through that wall of Chinese troops. If the Marines defended, they would be wiped out. So they formed a twelve-mile long column and attacked.

There were seventy-eight miles of narrow, crumbling, steeply angled road and 100,000-plus Chinese soldiers between the Marines and the sea at Hungnam. Both sides fought savagely for every inch of it. The march out became one monstrous moving battle.

The Chinese used the ravines between ridges because it was necessary to protect themselves from rifle fire, and to allow them to marshal their forces between attacks. The Marine's 60 mm mortars, capable of delivering high, arcing fire over the ridgelines to break up those human waves, became perhaps the most valuable weapon the Marines had. But their supply of mortar rounds was quickly depleted. Emergency requests for resupply were sent by radio, using code words for specific items. The code for 60 mm mortar ammo was "Tootsie Rolls" but the radio operator receiving that urgent request didn't have the Marine's code sheets. All he knew was that request came from command authority, it was extremely urgent and there were tons of Tootsie Rolls (the candy) at the supply bases in Japan.

Tootsie Rolls had been issued with other rations for US troops since World War I, but they were cold and hard and required different handling compared to other candies.

Tearing through the clouds and fog, parachutes bearing pallet loads of Tootsie Rolls descended on the Marines. After an initially shocked reaction, the freezing, starving troops rejoiced since the only food they'd had was snow. Frozen Tootsie Rolls were thawed in armpits, popped in mouths, and the sugar provided instant energy. For many of the Marines, Tootsie Rolls were their only nourishment for days. The troops also learned they could use warmed Tootsie Rolls to plug bullet holes in fuel drums, gas tanks, cans, and radiators, where they would freeze solid again, sealing the leaks.

Over two weeks of unspeakable misery, movement, and murderous fighting, the fifteen-thousand-man column suffered three thousand killed in action, six thousand wounded, and thousands of severe frostbite cases. But they reached the sea, demolishing several

Chinese divisions in the process. Hundreds credited their survival to Tootsie Rolls. The surviving Marines were called "The Chosin Few," and among themselves they had another name: The Tootsie Roll Marines.

CHAPTER 31

ANGEL'S GATE

Many years ago, the survivors of the Frozen Chosin met at San Pedro, California, to honor the fallen Marines who gave their lives in Korea. The Governor of Nevada had issued and signed a proclamation for the fallen men who died in Korea. A few of us arranged to meet at the Angel's Gate in San Pedro, California, for the unveiling of a proposed statue for the Korean veterans. Angel's Gate sits on a high bluff overlooking the ocean. The memorial was to be by the "Freedom's Bell," a Korean monument that sits in a beautiful oriental pagoda with a breathtaking view overlooking the Pacific Ocean. The monument that we were going to dedicate was to be created by the same sculptor that had designed the Iwo Jima monuments in Washington, DC. Our job was to help raise the funds, but our efforts were cut short by the California Coastal Committee, who decided to cancel construction of the monument, due to their determination that it represented a war.

Bob Holtzer said it very well in his poem titled, "Angel's Gate."

> Out here on the Pacific Coast, you can hear the
>   ocean roar,
> As the waves from distant oceans pound the
>   Pacific shore,
> Up here on the hill is a spot that lays in wait,

For a tribute to our fallen at a place called "Angel's
  Gate."
"Korea" was the war our nation soon forgot,
Except for us veterans, we vowed that we would not!
It was many years ago when we marched off to war.
None of us knew then what we were fighting for.
We fought for Korea's freedom to live another day.
But our own nation forgot our men, "the dead
  and MIA."
We will give a proper tribute to our friends from
  long ago,
This international memorial to those guys we
  used to know.
No longer to be forgotten and never again to
  wait,
Let's pay homage to our fallen at this place called
  "Angel's Gate."

On the left side of the planned memorial mock-up was the
Nevada Proclamation, and on the right side was a rifle with a bayonet
stuck in the ground and a Marine Corps helmet on top. When the
group had gathered at Angels Gate to dedicate the area, we noticed
that an older lady had approached the rifle and placed her right hand
on top of the helmet as she looked out to sea. I walked up beside her
and asked her why she was standing there with her hand on the helmet. She replied that she was from South Korea, and that she was a
young lady when this historic war took place. She recalled her memories about the train depot, and the war, and she said that if it were
not for the US Marines she would not be here today. She said that
she had seen and heard what was planned for Korea, and that all her
family had been killed by the North Korean Army. She had hidden
from them and had escaped, and she stated that the people of South
Korea would never forget how the United States saved her country
from the North Korea Communists.

CHAPTER 32

LETTERS HOME

September 15, 1950, Big day tomorrow
September 29, 1950, Town of Seoul
October 2, 1950, A hilltop in Korea
October 3, 1950, USS *Consolation*
October 6, 1950, Incheon
October 12, 1950, Incheon
October 15, 1950, Out to sea
October 18, 1950, Off the coast of Wonsan
October 29, 1950, USS *Consolation*
October 31, 1950, One day after surgery
November 5, 1950, No mail
November 10, 1950, Back on the beach
November 11, 1950, Wonsan
November 17, 1950, Hamhung
November 19, 1950, Hi, Twins and Betty
November 20, 1950, Thank you for the package
November 22, 1950, Thanksgiving
November 27, 1950, Chosin Reservoir
November 29, 1950, Chosin Reservoir
December 4, 1950, Chosin Reservoir
December 13, 1950, Hangnam
December 15, 1950, Out at sea
December 19, 1950, Mason
December 25, 1950, Mason

Sept 15, 1950

Dear Mom & Dad,

Well here I am writing again on my spare time, this wont be a long letter. Tomorrow is the big day for us you'll probly read all about it.

I'll tell you one thing I'll be glad to get off this garbage scow. We're riding out a nother typhone, thats why this writing is crude.

How is everyone at home, fine I hope, and how is Jim Dan & Luis say hi to them for me. What is the latest news back in the states. I'll try to write as offten as I can but this will be the last for now. Tell the twins to keep writing and also tell them thanks for the nice complement their girl friend said, even though it isn't true.

II

You should see me, I grew a mustach and do I look like a clown, ha ha!!

I dont know what I would do if I didn't recive any letters, what I been doing in the last 20 days would drive a man thats in his right mind crazy. And the worst is still to come.

Do you think you can send me some cookies or any thing.

Tell Dad to take it easy and not to wory about me, Ill be ok. Ill close this letter for now.

Lots of love & Kises to all
Ken

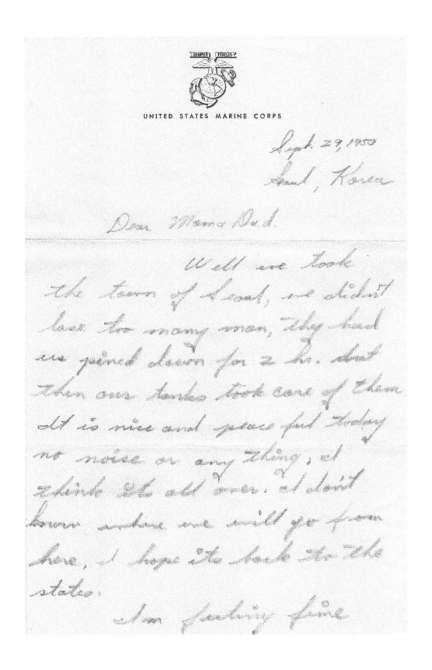

UNITED STATES MARINE CORPS

Sept. 29, 1950
Saul, Korea

Dear Mama Dad.

Well we took
the town of Seoul, we didn't
lose too many men, they had
us pined down for 2 hr. but
then our tanks took care of them
It is nice and peaceful today
no noise or any thing, I
think it's all over. I don't
know where we will go from
here, I hope its back to the
states.
I'm feeling fine

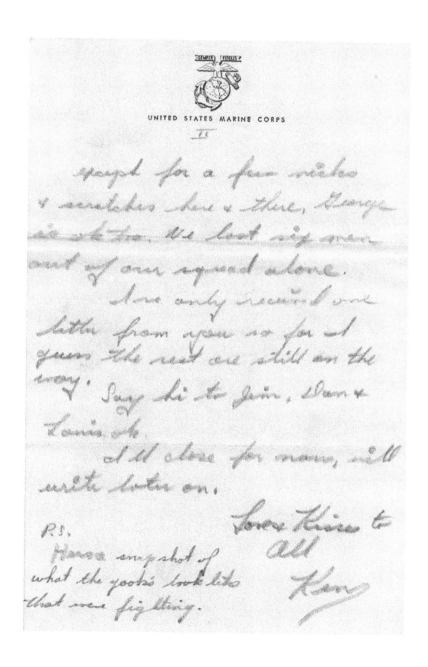

UNITED STATES MARINE CORPS

except for a few nicks & scratches here & there, George is ok too. We lost six men out of our squad alone.

I've only received one letter from you so far, I guess the rest are still on the way. Say hi to Jim, Dan & Louis etc.

I'll close for now, will write later on.

P.S.
Heres a snapshot of what the gooks look like that were fighting.

Love & Kisses to All

Ken

Oct 2, 1950
On a hilltop in
Korea.

Dear Mom & Dad,
Received your letter
yesterday on the 1st it was post
marked on the 19th of Sept. your
still forgetting to put "C" Co. on
it.

Glad to hear that everyone
at home is ok, as for my self
I'm feeling fine. The weather
over here is just like calif.
its hot in the day time and
cold at night.

Did the kids get the stuff
I sent them.

So Louis is going to school
now, how does he like it. He'll
get used to it.

Wish Uncle Mike, Albert
& Jim a happy birthday for me
ok.

II

We haven't been doing any thing since we took Seoul, our company was the first to take and go through Seoul, it sure was a hot battle. These gooks over here have no regards for human life, and if any body gets in the way they just shot them down.

I been receiving your letters but there getting mixed up becaus your not putting (" le on it

George is ok, Bill Ziegler just came back to the out fit, I don't even see why he went back all he had was a few schrapnel in his neck.

Well Mom & Dad I better close for now, say hi to Jim Allen & Louis and the rest of the family.

Love & Kisses to All
Ken

Oct 3, 1950
U.S.S. Consolation

Dear Mom & Dad,

Well here it is the third of Oct. gosh the days & months are sure going by fast. the situation look's pretty bad the doggies are starting to run back now & the Chinese Com. are sticking there nose in it. I sure wish they would give up. I've had my share of war & fighting but it looks as if I'm going to have more.

The doc. took the stiches out of my face & the swelling is going down, it

II

won't be long now & I'll be just like new. I just heard on the radio that some one tried to shot Truman, whats the matter with the people back there in the states were having enough trouble over here with out them starting something back there.

I've been talking to some guys that just came in & they said that George was pickedup by heolecaptor & that he is ok. thats just rumors, I'll find out when I get back.

Well I'll close for now.

Love & kisses to All

Ken

P.S.
Say hi to Jim
Don & Louis

Oct. 6, 1950
Inchon, Korea

Dear Mom & Dad,

Sorry I havn't written in the last few day, but we are now back at Inchon at a rest camp & awaiting to board ship's. Where were going from here I don't know, I guess it all depends on the situation up north but I hope it back to the states. I have a nice souvenier to take home, it's a machine tripod with a beautiful bullet hole in it. It was ment for me but I guess the prayer's I've been saying that made it miss me. All it did was a take a few pieces of skin with it. No I don't get the purple heart.

Boy it sure does ful funny to be here sitting down

II

writting this letter in peace,
with out jumping every few
min. for a fox hole. "yes sir".
I sure will be glad to get back
to the states.

Glad to hear that every
one is fine at home & as for my self
I feel greate. I received your
letter that was dated the 1st of Oct.
it only took six days to get here
thats pretty fast don't you think.

So your going to buy a
T.V. set's huh, hope its a nice one.

Oh yes tell Dad not to
worry, I was only fooling about taking
a "nip" girl back to the states.

Don't send any more packages
untill I ask for one ok, because I
don't know weither Im going to stay
here or what.

I'll close for now so take
it easy & tell Dad not to work to hard.

Love & Kisses to All

Ken,

Oct. 12, 1950
Inchon, Korea

Dear Mom & Dad,

Received the letter
that the twins & Betty wrote me,
tell them I haven't much time to
write to them but I'll try.
You should be getting
a letter from the Gov. about me,
about the same time you get this.
Also a "Letter of Commendation" from
the Commendate of the Marine Corps
to me. Don't through it away, I
guess I'm a little hero so they tell
me, ha ha what a laugh, Don't let
it out.
Well were still in Inchon
waiting for further orders from the U.N.
council, hope its back to the states.

Oh yes! I cant understand

II

Why the twins didn't receive
the stuff I sent them. oh well
may be the mail is just slow.
    Received a nother letter
from Kish. ~~is he still going~~
to school, hope he makes good.
    Did you hear any thing
about the extra year were suppose
to spend in the service.
    Am running short of
words so I'll stop for now

                    Love & Kisses to All

                            Ken

P.S.
Say hi to Jim
Dan & Louis.

Oct. 15, 1950
Putting out to sea.

Dear Mom & Dad,

Well were back aboard ships again, and were pulling out of Inchon with intentions of going up north. Just think one month ago we were just come landing here. And here it is one month later & were moving up north, I guess we have to go up there and help those doggies again.

How does the situation look to you people back in the states. Has there been any write ups in the paper about "C" Co. 1st Mar.

We've seen more combat then the other two company's and yet we have less casulties. We've lost twelve men alone from our machine gun plt. and that's pretty light.

Have you received any letters concerning me from the Gov. Our Co. was called together and they gave us a big speech on how greate a job we done, and to the men in the co. that rated metals he gave us a nother speech, I don't know what I've done. but I guess if it was any one else he would of done the same. And as far as being called a hero, I don't want to be called one. So when that letter comes keep it under your hat. Oot yes did the twins get the package yet. How are the kids. I'm sending a Korean Wan it takes 2,500 Won to make up one american dollar. Tell the twins to save it for me. I also have a couple of South Korean flags & a couple of Northe Koreans Commenist flag's. I had a gook's ear but it rotted away so I guess I'll just have to get some gold teeth ha'ha! I'll close for now, don't forget to write often.

Love & Kisses to All

Kens.

AMERICAN RED CROSS

Oct. 18, 1950
Off the coast of
Wonsan, Korea

Dear Mom & Dad,

Well here it
is Wed, and its our third day
out. So far were having good
weather, the weather over here
is just like Calif.

How is everyone at
home, fine I hope, As for
myself I'm ok.

It look like this
war will last a couple of
more weeks or longer &
there when its over, I don't
know what were going
to do.

How are the kids doing in school. Did the aloutment start to come in yet. By the time I get back I should have g a good start in the bank. Are you going to put it in the bank for me.

When I get out I think I'll go back to night school on the G.I. Bill, what do you think.

Think ill close for now.

Love & Kisses to all
Ken

AMERICAN RED CROSS

Oct. 29, 1950
U.S.S. Constellation

Dear Mom & Dad,

This is my first chance to write since we hit the beach.

I hope you aint worrying about me, Im ok. The gooks pulled a Banzi attack on us the 27 of Oct at one A.M. and I was hit with two fragmation grenades. They were trying to knock out my machine gun position but it took

AMERICAN RED CROSS

but it took three grenades
The first one missed me, the
second one got me in the
left arm & the third one blew
up in my face. I don't
know why I'm not dead
I guess its because Gods on
my side.

The grenade that
blew up in my face
threw a few chunk of
schrapnal, one hit me under
the left eye & the other

AMERICAN RED CROSS
II

hit me under the right
eyes, giving me a beautiful
black eye. the doctor says
they won't even leave a scar.

this is going to be a
shock to you as it was to
me when I found out, George
Kinnick is missing, knew one
no's where he is either he was
taken prisoner or else he
is running around in the hills.
I hope & pray to God that
they find him alive.

AMERICAN RED CROSS

IV

So don't worry about me. I'll be ok.

I'm going to close for now so I can get some sleep.

Love & Kisses to All

Ken

P.S.

Say hello to Jim, Dan & Lauri & also the twins & Betty. Tell Dad not to worry.

+
AMERICAN RED CROSS

Oct. 31, 1950
U.S.S. Consutation

Dear Mom & Dad.

Though I'd drop
you a few lines, seing that
im feeling better today. The
Doc. operated on my face yesterday
and he said that the schrapnel
will have to stay in my face
he said it was two close to
my eyes & besides it right
near the nurve that it controls
my face muscles, he also
said that it wouldnt

give me any trouble in
later life so I guess I
got a couple of souveniers, ha ha
the one under my left eye
is 5x5 mm & the one under
my right one is a 1x5 mm, that's
pretty good size.

I still haven't heard
any thing about George, I
just hope they find him.

How are all the kids
say hi to Jim Don & Louis
for me, also how is H.L &

✚
AMERICAN RED CROSS

& Pat and thier new
born baby & Terry.
I don't know when
I'm going back to duty I
hope it is for a couple of
more day's.
Well Mom & Dad
i'll close for now.

Love & Kisses to All

Ken

Nov. 5, 1950
U.S.S. Consolation

Dear Mom & Dad,

Well here it is
the 5th of Nov. and I haven't
received any mail from you or
any one else since the 14th
of Oct. I guess it hasn't
caught up with me yet.

The latest news on
George is good. He's ok but
the poor kid went through
hell for two night and
two days. He was up in
the mountains by him self

II

with no chow. Just to
tell you how lucky he was,
a gook officer + about 10 or
15 other gooks walked within
three feet of him & never even
seen him, he waited until they
passed and then he decided
to get out of there. He ran for
2 ½ miles without stopping
they said he was so harried
that he couldn't even open
his chow cans. But the main
thing is that he is safe +
unhurt. I also said a prayer
to God thanking him for

III

watching over him.

Am feeling pretty good
in fact I dread going back
to the beach. I heard that
my outfit moved up north.
Boy is it <u>cold</u> over here.

Well mom & dad I close
for now. Here's hoping I
receive some mail soon.

Love & Kisses
to all
Kenny

P.S.

Say hi to Jim
Dan & Louie

Nov. 10, 1950
Wonsan Korea

Dear Mom & Dad,

Well I'm back on the beach again, but I still wish I was on the ship. Boy is it cold!

Well today was a big day for us, as you know today is the Marine Corps birthday & they had a big ceremony and they gave me my Purple Heart. I'll try to send it home.

How is every one at home

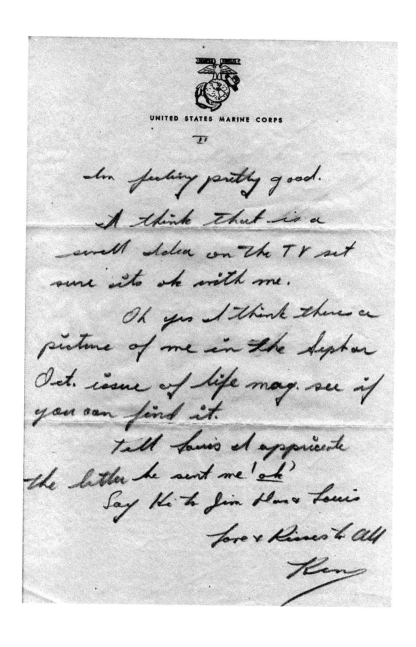

UNITED STATES MARINE CORPS

Im feeling pretty good.

I think that is a swell idea on the TV set sure its ok with me.

Oh yes I think there a picture of me in the Septor Oct. issue of life mag. see if you can find it.

tell Louis I appreciate the letter he sent me 'ok'

Say Hi to Jim Stan & Louis

Love & Kisses to All

Ken

Nov. 11, 1950
Wonsan, Korea

Dear Mom & Dad,

It's pretty warm today so I decided i'd write a few lines while it's still hot.

We're protecting an air base here in Wonsan, the Army is finaly begaining to like us. They should, after we pulled them out of holes & etc.

I guess you read about the ambush the gooks pulled on the 1st Mar, well it was our outfit down at Kojo, about 35 —

II

miles south from Wonsan, that was when I got hit.

The Chaplain was up here today and said that there was a mass tomorrow & if we didn't go, he was going to shoot us ha ha.

How is every one at home, I fine & so is George. Say hello to Jim Dune Louis

Love & Kisses to All

Kenz

Nov. 17, 1950
Hamhung, Korea.

Dear Mom & Dad.

Well I finly got some stationary to write a letter, we moved up to Hamhung, three days ago. The weather up here is miserable, just to let you know how cold it is, the water in our canteens froze last night & I think the temperature was down to 10° & that too cold for me.

How is every one at home fine I hope as for me im feeling fine except I tired

II

of this war, & killing
people so they won't kill me.
And I'm tired of sleeping in holes
and eating out of cans & going for
weeks without washing up. I
just hope & pray to God to end
this war.

I haven't received any mail
since Oct. 13, I wonder whats
happening to them.

I'll close this short letter
for know untill next time.

P.S.   Love & Kisses to All
Say hello to Jim   Ken
Dan & Louis.

Nov. 19, 1950

Humhung, Korea

Hi twins + Betty.

Well I'm finly getting around to answer your letters.

I glad to hear that you liked your gifts. I just guessed the size. Did Betty like the jacket, she can wore it when she go's to a skating rink or etc.

I think you should ware those jagamas to the "Fiesta" you might win he he.

You wanted to know if the people over here can speak English, No. maybe 1 out of a thousand can speak it & then its no good.

II

When you get a chance
take a picture of your self
in those pj & send it to
me ok.

There isn't much to tell
you about any thing over here,
except the people are very poor
and they live in houses made
out of mud. It's very cold
over here, the night before last
it rained & we (George & I) slept
in two foot of water were we
wet & cold.

Well kids I'll close
for now. Dont forget to write

Ken

Nov. 22, 1950
Hamhung Korea

Dear Mom & Dad,

I had a few spare moments & I thought I'd write a few lines. Tomorrow is Thanksgiving & were moving up north 30 or 40 miles. I guess were going to the reservoirs or else to the border. Theirs a rumor going around that were going to stay here for the winter, our intelligence said that there is 193 days of sub zero weather, we have reports now that it get 20 or 30° bellow zero here thats cold. Hope I can survive.

How is everyone at home and how is the weather over there in the states still cool,

II

I'm sure going to miss being home for the thanksgiving dinner, I don't think will get any. We prably will get 'C' ration & there no good.

I received a letter from Rich & he I said that color T.V. is out. Why don't you get Dad one of those or are thy to expensive.

I sure wish I had a camara over here, I could of taken a lot of pictures, that would make the comment back there in the states think twice.

I close for now & drop you a couple of more lines when we get to our new position

Love & Kisses to All

Ken

P.S.
Say hello to
Jim Dan & Louis

Nov. 27, 1950
Chosen Reservoir
Korea.

Dear Mom & Dad.

Well Im finely getting around to writing you a few lines. Before I say any thing else it cold over here so far the lowest its been is 14° below 0° + I liked to have froze.

Recived a letter from Al. sure was good to hear from him, glad to hear that every thing is ok with him & the family. He also said that they have the xmas trees up on Hollywood Blvd. Sure would of liked to seen

II

the X Mass parade.

How is everyone at home fine I hope as for me I'm fine.

We got a stove in our tent and it sure helps out. Because it gets cold around day break. We have a stream running by our tent & its all frozen.

Were guarding a ammo dump up here & how long will be here I don't know.

The last letter I received from you was dated the 13th & I think I answered it.

Also heard that Tony's wife had a baby boy & also Frank & the dyp. my God every one is having kids ha ha.

III

It's funny when you start to write a letter you always have a lot to say, but once you get a pen in your hand you forget what your going to say. So i'll close for now.

Love & Kisses to All

Ken

P.S.
Say hello to Jim Don & Lou ok.

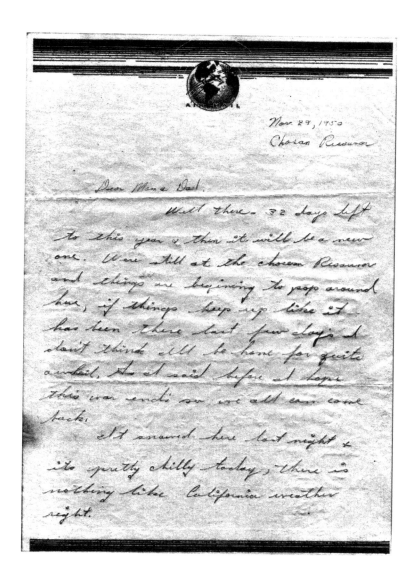

Nov 27, 1950
Chosin Reservoir

Dear Mom & Dad,

Well there - 32 days left to this year & then it will be a new one. We're still at the Chosin Reservoir and things are beginning to peep around here, if things keep up like it has been these last few days I don't think I'll be here for quite awhile. As I said before I hope this war ends so we all can come back.

It snowed here last night & its pretty chilly today, there is nothing like California weather right.

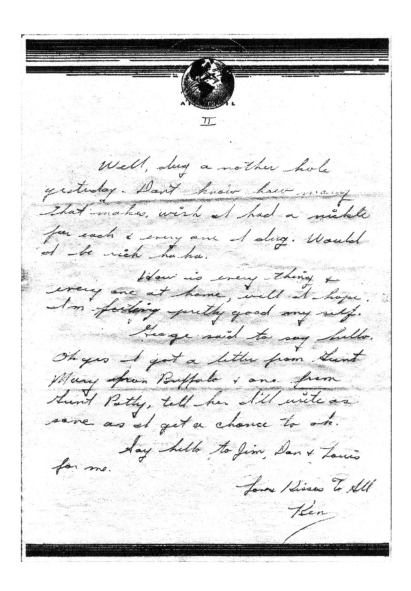

Well, dug a nother hole yesterday. Dont know how many that makes, wish I had a nickle for each & every one I dug. Would I be rich ha ha.

How is every thing & every one at home, will I hope. Am feeling pretty good my self.

Geage said to say hello. Oh yes I got a letter from Aunt Mary from Buffalo & one from Aunt Patty, tell her I'll write as soon as I get a chance to ok.

Say hello to Jim, Dan & Louis for me.

Love / Kisses To All

Ken

Dec. 4, 1950
Chosin Reservoir

Dear Mom & Dad,

Well here it is the 4th of Dec. and only 21 days to Christmas. Sure wish I could be home.

How is everyone at home, I'm feeling pretty good. Yesterday was the first time I washed up in three weeks, & boy was it dirty.

I received a letter from Phillama, and from what she says, there doing pretty good. Also there planing a trip to Buffalo for Christmas

The gooks ambushed our mail truck, now they cant find the driver or the truck. Boy that makes me mad.

II

Today is Georges birthday, so he want have to do any work; lucky day.

We dug a hole 12' x 12' and 3' deep and then lined them with sand bags. Then we put a roof on, made um self a little store, et pretty warm.

The wind is really blowing hard today.

How are all the kids say hi to them for me. I'll close for now. until next time.

Love & Kisses to All

Ken.

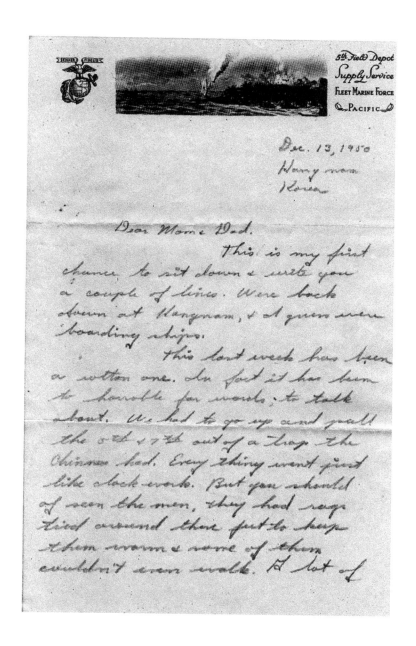

5th Field Depot
Supply Service
Fleet Marine Force
Pacific

Dec. 13, 1950
Hungnam
Korea

Dear Mom & Dad,

This is my first chance to sit down & write you a couple of lines. Were back down at Hungnam, & I guess were boarding ships.

This last week has been a rotten one. In fact it has been to horrible for words; to talk about. We had to go up and pull the 5th & 7th out of a trap the Chinese had. Every thing went just like clock work. But you should of seen the men, they had rags tied around there feet to keep them warm & some of them couldn't even walk. A lot of

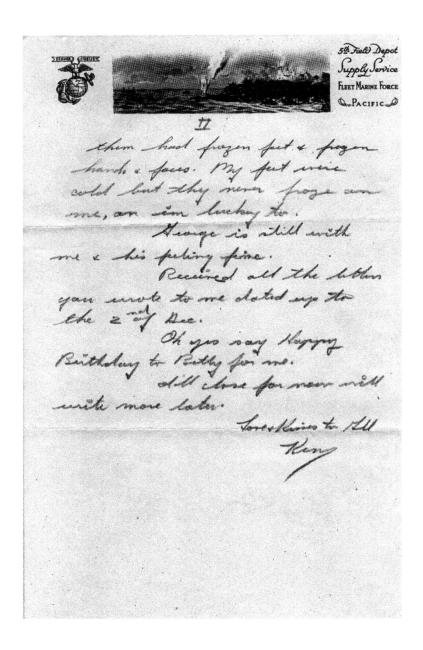

them had frozen feet & frozen
hands & faces. My feet were
cold but they never froze on
me, an im lucky to.

George is still with
me & his feeling fine.

Received all the letters
you wrote to me dated up to
the 2nd of Dec.

Oh yes say Happy
Birthday to Ruthy for me.

I'll close for now will
write more later.

Love & Kisses to All

Ken

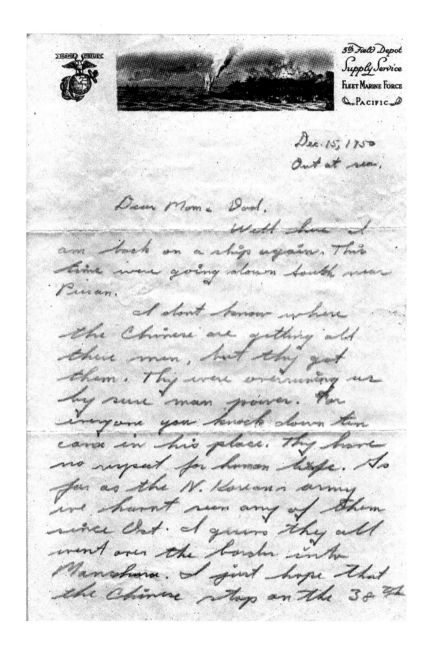

5th Field Depot
Supply Service
Fleet Marine Force
Pacific

Dec. 15, 1950
Out at sea.

Dear Mom & Dad,
Well here I
am back on a ship again. This
time were going down south near
Pusan.
I don't know where
the Chinese are getting all
these men, but they got
them. They were overrunning us
by sure man power. For
everyone you knock down ten
came in his place. They have
no respect for human life. As
far as the N. Korean army
we havn't seen any of them
since Oct. I guess they all
went over the border into
Manchuria. I just hope that
the Chinese stop on the 38th

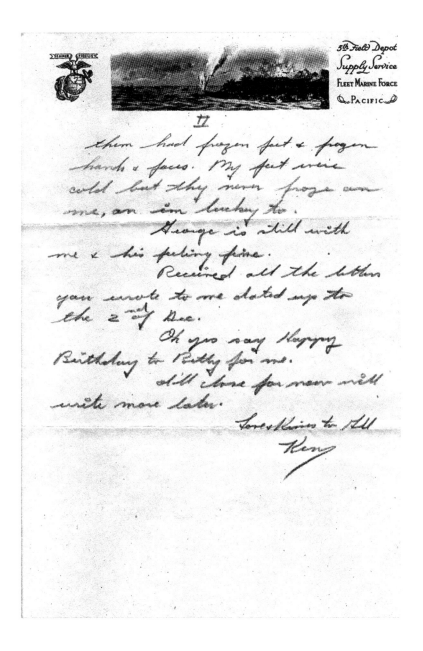

them had frozen feet & frozen
hands & faces. My feet were
cold but they never froze on
me, an im lucky to.
George is still with
me & his feeling fine.
Received all the letters
you wrote to me dated up to
the 2nd of Dec.
Oh yes say Happy
Birthday to Ruthy for me.
ill close for now will
write more later.
Lovekisses to All
Ken

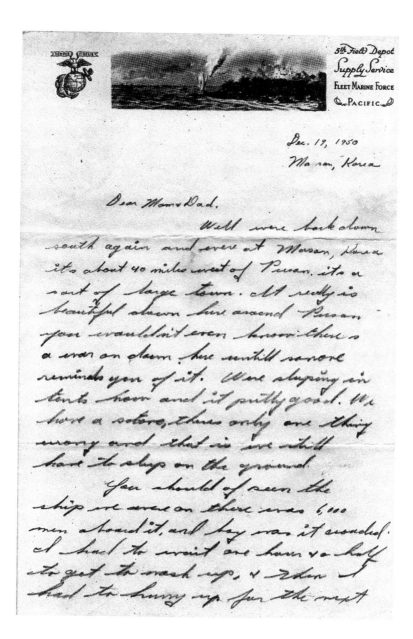

5th Field Depot
Supply Service
FLEET MARINE FORCE
PACIFIC

Dec. 19, 1950
Masan, Korea

Dear Mom & Dad,

Well were back down south again and ever at Masan, Korea its about 40 miles west of Pusan. its a sort of large town. It really is beautiful down here around Pusan you wouldn't even know there's a war on down here untill someone reminds you of it. We're sleeping in tents here and it pretty good. We have a stove, theres only one thing wrong and that is we still have to sleep on the ground.

You should of seen the ship we were on there was 6,000 men aboard it, and boy was it crowded. I had to wait one hour & a half to get to wash up, & then I had to hurry up for the next

5th Field Depot
Supply Service
Fleet Marine Force
Pacific

guy. Then I decided I wanted to eat that mess. I got to eat at 01:30, there was a line a mile long. What a trip that was.

Oh yes I received a Christmas card from Aunt Pat & Uncle Mike it was very nice. I received your letter dated the eighth of Dec.

Yes it was our Div that was trapped by the reds. We weren't really trapped we just meet the enemy on all sides, but we pulled through with not to much loss on our sides. It was all the Army fault again.

I'd like to come home & I guess so would everyone else, but we cant. There's not enough of us over here now. Altogether the Chinks have about two million men over here now. And

overrunning us by shure man
power, you knock one down &
10 come back in his place how
can you fight some one like
that. This war is just like a
foot ball game. We didn't want to
pull out by the Army ordered us
so we had nothing else to say.
Just think ill be 20 years
old next mounth. Well I hope
ill be home for my next birthday.
Haw are all the kids, say
hello to Jim Dan & Lewis.
Ill close for now untill
next time

Love kisses to all
Ken

5th Field Depot
Supply Service
Fleet Marine Force
Pacific

Dec. 25, 1950
Masan, Korea

Dear Mom & Dad,

Am awful sorry for not writing to you sooner. Received your letters dated up till the 15th. Also received a Xmas card from Rich.

Well I hope every one had a wonderful Xmas we had a pretty good meal I sent you the menue that we had for dinner

How is everyone at home fine I hope as for myself I still have a little cold, I just can't seem to get rid of it. The weather down here is a little warmer then

it was up north.
Do you Rember Frank
White, I brough him home
one, well he was hit in
both knees, a piece of schrop
nel went into his chin &
came out of his nose, and
another piece hit him in
his left hand, he'll never
be able to use it again
because its paralyze. It
sure was a shock to hear
about it. George is okey

You say the weather is
nice & warm now I sure
would of liked to been home
for XMas & I sure do miss
the states & white people.
Its going on 5 mo. that
Ive been over here & it
seem like five years to
me.

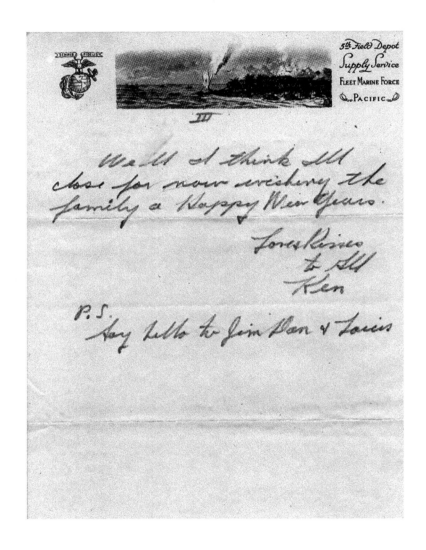

Well I think I'll
close for now wishing the
family a Happy New Years.

Love Kisses
to All
Ken

P.S.
Say hello to Jim Dan & Louis

CHAPTER 33

KOREAN WAR SOUVENIRS

Magazine and Newspaper Clippings

On a hill overlooking the fighting zone, Gen. MacArthur confers with Marine Col. Lewis B. Puller (l.) and Vice-Adm. A. D. Struble

RED DRIVES FORCE ALLIES BACK—U.S. troops on Korea west coast have been forced to withdraw 50 miles south and east to Chongju (1), while Reds pushing down from Unsan area (2) knifed closer to Kunu in offensive to trap two 1st Cavalry Division regiments. Marines jumping off from Sudong in drive on Changjin reservoir (3) were threatened with encirclement by flank attacks. South Koreans made slight gains past Kilchu (4) on east coast. By-passed Reds (5) were attacking near Wonsan.
(AP Wirephoto map)

KOREA WAR

Continued from First Page

were two divisions operating in the area.

In the northeast section alone, two Chinese Red divisions were reported in action. But this is the first official confirmation of that number of Chinese troops in Korea.

United Nations forces still were holding some positions near Unsan, 20 miles north of Kunu. The South Korean 1st Division, seven miles south of Unsan, was under attack from 5 p.m. Friday until midnight.

A North Korean communique asserted that the Reds have killed or wounded 1500 U.N. officers and men and taken 2000 prisoners "in the Anju area," 15 miles southwest of Kunu.

Aided by Planes

The marine regiment which got into trouble in northeast Korea yesterday was advancing near Sudong, 20 miles northwest of the east coast industrial city of Hamhung.

A marine briefing officer said

100,000 BARRELS OF OIL are stacked on shore at Point Molate Navy Fuel Annex, Richmond, Calif. Out at the end of the pier two tankers are taking on fuel

IN TOKYO 34½ hours after leaving San Francisco, Marines line up on the runway and get rifles ready for inspection. They will leave for Korea almost at once.

IN PUSAN HARBOR thousands of drums of machine oil, gasoline and jet fuel, unloaded from MSTS cargo ships, are stock-piled for transshipment to the front. With new shipments of oil and gas coming into Korea each week, the stock pile is rapidly being built up to handle the huge demands of the coming U.S. offensive.

THE TOOTSIE ROLL MARINES

Korea War Casualties

3 From So. Cal. Killed in Action

Sixteen Southern Californians, including three killed in action, were named today in a new Department of Defense casualty list. They were:

KILLED IN ACTION

Pfc. Henry H. Ascencio, army, son of Mrs. Amalia H. Ascencio, Camarillo.

Staff Sergeant Robert J. Kikta, Marine Corps, husband of Mrs. Robert J. Kikta, 1913-F Tarawa street, Building 69, Sterling Housing, Oceanside.

Capt. Talvin J. Roraus, air force, husband of Mrs. Patricia C. Roraus, 4269 Sawtelle boulevard, Culver City. (Previously reported missing in action.)

WOUNDED

Pfc. Robert W. Baker, army, son of Mrs. Arminta A. Baker, 1611 West Fourth street, Los Angeles.

Pfc. Rodolfo Casas, army, son of Mrs. Isabel Rodrigues Casas, 946½ North Vignes street, Los Angeles.

Corporal Rodolfo R. Hernandez, army, nephew of Mrs. Victoria Dominquez, 211 Mary avenue, Calexico.

Pvt. Graviel A. Lucero, army, son of Mrs. Francisca A. Lucero, 12011 Elnidale street, Norwalk.

Cpl. Louis P. Stelman, army, son of Mrs. Emily M. Steelman, 5011 West 141st street, Hawthorne.

Cpl. Gerald R. Thompson, army, son of Mrs. Juanita D. Thompson, 1354 219th street, Torrance.

Cpl. Robert W. Woodruff, army, son of Mrs. Anna Nicolette, 6517 Foster Bridge street, Bell Gardens.

Pfc. Robert R. Eggleston, Marine Corps, son of Mr. and Mrs. Eddie H. Eggleston, 948 East Century boulevard, Los Angeles.

First Lieut. John K. McLeod, Marine Corps, husband of Mrs. John K. McLeod, 257½ Nieto, Long Beach.

Sgt. Manuel Mota, Marine Corps, son of Mr. and Mrs. Felicinao Mota, General Delivery, Gonzales.

Pfc. Kenneth F. Santor, Marine Corps, son of Mr. and Mrs. Albert C. Santor, 321 East Elm street, Compton.

INJURED

Pfc. John B. Doughty, army, son of Mrs. Frances G. Doughty, 612 F. avenue, National City.

MISSING IN ACTION

Pvt. Paul Mason, army, son of Mrs. Flora Mason, Tagus Ranch, Tulare.

IWO JIMA HERO WOUNDED IN KOREA

Capt. Harold G. Schrier (inset) of Chilson, N. Y., has been wounded in Korean fighting. He was one of little band of marines pictured in immortal photo above raising American flag on Mount Saribachi, Iwo Jima, in World War II.

Iwo Jima

Member of Flag Epic Wounded in Korea

By Associated Press

WASHINGTON, Jan. 10.—One of the famous little band of marines who raised the flag on Mount Saribachi, Iwo Jima, is a casualty of the Korean War.

A casualty list issued today contained the name of Capt. Harold G. Schrier of Chilson, N. Y. He is wounded.

Schrier, then a first lieutenant, led a 40-man patrol up Suribachi on Feb. 23, 1945. He is one of the seven men, five of whom show distinctly, in the historic photograph made by Joe Rosenthal, then an Associated Press photographer.

Of the seven men at the flag-raising ceremony, four subsequently were killed in action in World War II.

13 Southland Casualties

Names of service men from Southern California appear on the latest casualty list from the Korean war zone released yesterday by the Department of Defense.

They are:

KILLED IN ACTION
ARMY
PFC Henry H. Ascencio, son of Mrs. Amalia Ascencio, Camarillo.
MARINE CORPS
S/Sgt. Robert J. Kitka, husband of Mrs. Robert Kitka, Oceanside.
AIR FORCE
Capt. Talvin J. Roraus, husband of Mrs. Patricia Roraus, 4269 Sawtelle boulevard, Culver City. (Previously reported missing in action.)

WOUNDED
ARMY
PFC Robert W. Baker, son of Mrs. Arminta Baker, 1611 West Fourth street, Los Angeles.

PFC Rodolfo Casas, son of Mrs. Rodriguez Casas, 946½ North Vignes street, Los Angeles.

Pvt. Graviel A. Lucero, son of Mrs. Francisca Lucero, 12011 Elindale street, Norwalk.

Pvt. Louis P. Steelman, son of Mrs. Emily M. Steelman, 5011 West 141st street, Hawthorne.

Cpl. Gerald R. Thompson, son of Mrs. Juanita D. Thompson, Torrance.

Cpl. Robert W. Woodruff, son of Mrs. Anna Nicolette, Bell Gardens.

MARINE CORPS
Pfc. Robert R. Eggleston, son of Mrs. Eddie Eggleston, 948 East Century boulevard, Los Angeles.

First Lieut. John K. McLeod, husband of Mrs. John K. McLeod, Long Beach.

Pfc. Kenneth F. Santor, son of Mr. and Mrs. Albert C. Santor, Compton.

INJURED
ARMY
Pfc. John B. Doughty, son of Mrs. Francis G. Doughty, National City.

Los Angeles Examiner

Richard A. Carrington Jr., Publisher
VOL. XLVII.   SUNDAY, NOV. 12.   No. 236
Daily and Sunday. Reg. U. S. Pat. Office. Examiner Building, 1111 S. Broadway. Postal Unit, Los Angeles 54, California. Published by Hearst Publishing Company, Inc., a Delaware corporation.
Entered as second-class matter, December 12, 1903, at the post office at Los Angeles, Calif., under the Act of March 3, 1879.
The Los Angeles Examiner Is Not Responsible for Unsolicited Manuscripts or Photographs. None will be returned unless sender incloses return postage.
BY CARRIER IN CALIFORNIA
Daily and Sunday ...... 46c per week
Daily and Sunday .... $2.00 per month
Sunday only ...... 15c per issue
MAIL RATES PAYABLE IN ADVANCE
IN CALIFORNIA
Daily and Sunday, one month $2.00
Daily without Sunday, one month....1.60
Sunday only, one month ...... .75
OTHER STATES
Daily and Sunday, one month, mail.. 2.20
Daily and Sunday, one month, carrier 2.60
Daily without Sunday, one month... 1.95
Sunday only, one month ... 1.00
FOREIGN COUNTRIES
Daily and Sunday, one month ... 3.75
Daily without Sunday, one month... 3.00
Sunday only, each ... .35
Air Mail, above rates plus air service cost.
MEMBER OF THE ASSOCIATED PRESS
The Associated Press is entitled exclusively to the use for republication of all the local news printed in this newspaper as well as all AP news dispatches.
SUBSCRIPTION COUPON
Los Angeles Examiner,
1111 S Broadway, Los Angeles, Calif.
Please enter my subscription for the

Examiner for_____months.

Name_____

Address_____

City and State_____

Inclosed is remittance $_____
☐ Daily and Sunday.
☐ Daily only.
☐ Sunday only.

239

★ ★ ★

A MARINE CHRISTMAS CARD

We kneeled to pray, this night
In Korea.
I turned and said, "Pray for the dead,"
This night:
And then the light burst on us,
In Korea.
We turned, and looked—a star shell!
So what to hell—let 'em snipe tonight,
In Korea . . .
We should give a damn!
But was it shell? Or star of Bethlehem,
This night,
That shone upon we praying few
In Korea.
That shone upon the silent dead,
Who to themselves had said,
"Dear Christ," and died,
In Korea.
Died that we might live,
And sing "Silent Night" in our silent hearts,
And look to Christ again
To bring hope to men, this night
In Korea.

★ ★ ★

—Associated Press Wirephoto

YANKS VIEW MONASTERY WRECKED BY REDS

Marines view wrecked interior of St. Benedict's Monastery, a Catholic mission and school six miles north of Wonsan, North Korea, after it had been smashed by Communist troops. Priests and nuns were among victims.

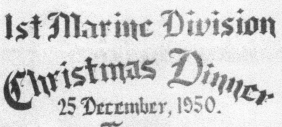

1st Marine Division
Christmas Dinner
25 December, 1950.
Korea
Menu

Shrimp Cocktail

Stuffed Olives   Sweet Pickles

Roast Young Tom Turkey

with

Cranberry Sauce	Giblet Dressing	Brown Gravy
	Creamed Corn	Wipped Potatoes
Green Beans	Glazed Sweet Potatoes	

Bread   Butter

Cole Slaw with Salad Dressing

Fruit Cake   Mincemeat Pie

Coffee

Hard Candies   Mixed Nuts

Fruit Salad

Cigarettes   Cigars

MERRY XMAS

North Korean Flag

WESTERN UNION

W. P. MARSHALL, PRESIDENT

CLASS OF SERVICE		SYMBOLS	
This is a full-rate Telegram or Cablegram unless its deferred character is indicated by a suitable symbol above or preceding the address.		DL = Day Letter	
		NL = Night Letter	
		LC = Deferred Cable	
		NLT = Cable Night Letter	
		Ship Radiogram	

The filing time shown in the date line on telegrams and day letters is STANDARD TIME at point of origin. Time of receipt is STANDARD TIME at point of destination

OA372 LG449

L.CPA134 RX GOVT PD=WUX WASHINGTON DC VIA COMPTON CALIF 1=

MR AND MRS ALBERT C SANTOR=

1235 HAGUE CT GLENDALE CALIF=

REGRET TO INFORM YOU THAT YOUR SON PRIVATE FIRST CLASS
KENNETH FRANCIS SANTOR USMC HAS BEEN WOUNDED IN ACTION 27
OCTOBER 1950 IN THE KOREAN AREA IN THE PERFORMANCE OF HIS
DUTY AND SERVICE OF HIS COUNTRY. I REALIZE YOUR GREAT
ANXIETY BUT NATURE OF WOUNDS NOT REPORTED AND DELAY IN
RECEIPT OF DETAILS MUST BE EXPECTED. YOU WILL BE PROMPTLY
FURNISHED ANY ADDITIONAL INFORMATION RECEIVED. HIS NEW
ADDRESS IS FIRST PROVISIONAL CASUAL COMPANY FMF FLEET POST
OFFICE SAN FRANCISCO CALIF=

C B CATES GENERAL USMC COMMANDANT OF THE MARINE CORPS=

THE COMPANY WILL APPRECIATE SUGGESTIONS FROM ITS PATRONS CONCERNING ITS SERVICE

Korean Flag signed by Machine Gunner Crew

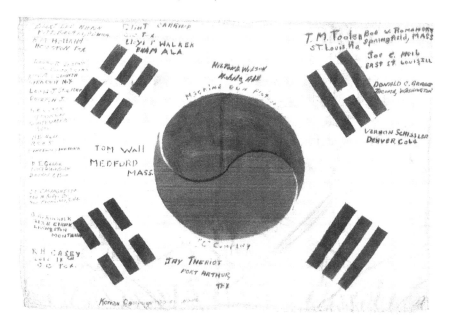

Headquarters   6/mpc
1st Marine Division FMF   1975
c/o FPO, San Francisco, Calif.

19 Dec 1950

DIVISION MEMORANDUM)
                     : Operations in the Chosin Reservoir Area
NUMBER.......238-50)

1. Early in November the First Marine Division launched a drive
from Hamhung toward the Chosin Reservoir. The 7th Marines, in
the lead, advanced north steadily and by agressive and determined
fighting finally decimated the 124th CCF Division in the vicinity
of Chinhung-ni. The advance continued to a point west of Yudam-ni,
when, on November 29th, due to the deteriorating situation on the
8th Army front and the appearance of several fresh Chinese
divisions in the Chosin Reservoir area, orders were received to
withdraw toward Hamhung. This withdrawal, which was concluded
when the last elements of the division closed the Hamhung area on
December 11th will become an epic in the annals of the Marine
Corps. Seldom, if ever, have Marines been forced to battle
against comparable odds. The enemy in overwhelming force was on
all sides, necessitating determined attacks to the front to clear
the way, resolute rear guard actions to keep the enemy from
closing in, and flank protection to guard the trains and the
wounded in the center of the column. Step by step the division
fought its way for a distance of thirty-five miles, always against
unremitting pressure from the enemy. First the 5th and 7th
Marines, with attached units, fought their way out of Yudam-ni,
over a 4,000 foot mountain pass and into Hagaru-ri. The losses
were heavy but the column was strengthened by the garrison at
Hagaru-ri, the 3d Battalion, 1st Marines, the 41st Royal Marine
Commandos, and Headquarters and Service units. Then the column
fought its way from Hagaru-ri to Koto-ri. Again losses were
heavy but the column was strengthened by the addition of the
headquarters of the 1st Marines, the 2d Battalion, 1st Marines,
and attached units then in garrison at Koto-ri. For the final
drive from Koto-ri to the relative security of Chinhung-ni at
the southern end of the tortuous mountain road below Koto-ri the
entire division participated. While the bulk of the division
fought down the mountain, the 1st battalion, 1st Marines fought
up the mountain to a juncture, thus permitting the trains to
descend the mountain with reasonable safety. Much of the road
over which this withdrawal was conducted was tortuous, narrow,
and snow-and ice-coated. Temperatures ranged from -5° to -20°F
imposing extreme hardship on men and causing considerable diff-
iculty with motor vehicles. There were road blocks, blown
bridges, and cratered roads. Yet in spite of determined enemy
resistance, hazardous roads and bitter weather the division
emerged from its ordeal a fighting division and inflicted heavy
casualties on the six enemy divisione encountered. All wounded
were evacuated, there were no stragglers, and useable equipment
was not destroyed except by enemy action.

2. The performance of officers and men in this operation was
magnificent. Rarely have all hands in a division participated

1

246

so intimately in the combat phases of an operation. Every
Marine can be justly proud of his participation. In Korea,
Tokyo and Washington there is full appreciation of the
remarkable feat of the division. With the knowledge of the
determination, professional competence, heroism, devotion to
duty, and self-sacrifice displayed by officers and men of this
division, my feeling is one of humble pride. No division
commander has ever been privileged to command a finer body of
men.

OLIVER P. SMITH
Major General, USMC
Commanding General,
1st Marine Division

DISTRIBUTION: To all members of the 1st Marine Division
and, and also Royal Marine Commandos.

HOSPITAL
Entertainment

By LINDA MANGELSDORF

READING A BOOK on the ceiling and turning the pages with your toes is just one man's way of taking advantage of the Special Services mobile library at the Tokyo Army Hospital.

Others are able to make more conventional utilization of the daily book service, covering the huge hospital's seven floors and the annexes.

Since its inauguration in 1946, the Special Services library has grown from a small collection of donated books—including 10 copies of "Little Lord Fauntleroy"—to a unit which can offer a variety of some 10,000 volumes.

But for Cpl. Tommy Hemby of Livingston, Tex., his push-button toe operation of the Special Services book projector was the answer to his reading problem.

"Lemme at 'em," he said, feinting with his bandaged mitts, as he flashed on another page of "Great American Sports."

A similar approach from other patients has been responsible for setting all-time highs in individual reading, according to Chief Librarian Kay Suzmann.

"And demands for 'OCS Material' have hit an all-time low," she said of the requests for comic books.

The problem of getting reading material to hundreds of bed patients —which has resulted in the tripling of the Special Services hospital library staff—is also a problem of catering to hundreds of different reading tastes.

Converted mess carts, equipped with shelves to carry 300 widely assorted books and magazines, have proved to be the solution. Each truck is manned by a library worker who, by covering the same wards daily, is able to compile a selection to meet the requests.

"There was only one boy I couldn't interest in books," said library worker Mrs. Virginia Russell. "And he wouldn't read because he was too busy knitting a red and yellow pair of argyle socks."

Not only are all the wards given daily book service, but the receiving tents, too, are serviced with expendable books and magazines as a volunteer project by Kay and her library workers.

In addition, individual reading projects of patients receive special consideration—even such ambitious projects as that of convalescent PFC Filomeno Farias of Los Angeles who announced in July that he was going to learn Russian and Japanese. Since then he has kept the library staff busy tracking down dictionaries and textbooks to keep up with his progress.

"At this rate, he'll be an interpreter by Thanksgiving," said assistant librarian Dorothy Pochel.

Rabid readers, such as PFC Ernest Gardner of Fort Worth, Tex., create another problem of supply. PFC Gardner's record of an average three books a day has covered a variety from "Anthony and Cleopatra" to "A Sub-Treasury of American Humor." His only plea has been to "keep 'em coming." And, according to the Special Services librarians, that is exactly what they plan to do.

CPL. TOMMY HEMBY of Livingston, Tex., demonstrates his toe dexterity to Special Services Chief Librarian, Kay Suzmann, at the Tokyo Army Hospital. (Photo by Tiers)

PFC EDDIE V. GREEN, Okamulgee, Okla.; PFC John H. Rowe, Mann, W. Va., and PFC Henry Cook, Philadelphia, Pa. receive books from Special Services assistant librarian Dorothy Pochel. (Photo by Tiers)

BEVERLY GAILLARD, Entertainment-Music technician, entertains liberated prisoners of war at Zama's 128th Station Hospital.

LT. JOSEPH V. GUILFOILE, popular pianist in Tokyo-Yokohama, entertains at the Tokyo Army Hospital during off-duty hours.

CPL. GENEVIEVE HARRIS, of Atlanta, Ga., entertains in hospital wards during her off-duty hours from her assignment at Hqs., JLC.

WOUNDED United Nations troops listen to Larry Dahms of New York City at Tokyo's Army General Hospital.

By SFC RAYMOND GILYARD

WHEN THE FIRST casualties from Korea arrived at local Army hospitals, American theatrical performers in Tokyo and Yokohama were ready, willing and able to contribute their talents to entertain the patients and bring a little something from home to wounded bed-ridden soldiers.

Under the management of Yokohama Command's Special Services Entertainment-Music Branch, performers are once again doing ward shows, playing for ambulatory patients in hospitals and appearing before vast audiences in troop staging areas —continuing a tradition established by members of the show world during World War II.

To coordinate acts, arrange transportation, provide technical assistance when needed, secure accompanists and execute a multitude of behind-the-scene chores, a central booking office was immediately established by the Entertainment-Music Branch.

Doreen McLean, Yokohama Command's theatrical adviser, became the guiding spirit behind what she labeled, "Operation Show-time." Although her office at times resembles an old fashioned vaudeville booking headquarters, with the constant jangling of phones, Miss McLean claims it really isn't as hectic as it seems. The former Broadway actress who has been associated with Army entertainment since her arrival in Japan in 1946, saw the need for hospital performances at the outbreak of hostilities. She contacted artists in the central Japan area and organized them into units.

Wards were visited and surveyed with an idea to presenting shows, while valuable assistance was received from Red Cross personnel with years of experience in hospital recreation programs.

Among the first to volunteer their talents were 1st Lt. Joseph V. Guilfoile, Larry Dahms, WAC Cpl. Genevieve Harris, 1st Lt. Arthur Keeney, Beverly Gaillard, and Melody Jones, all of them professional entertainers in their own right.

(Continued on Page 13)

BIBLIOGRAPHY

Appleman, Roy E. *South to the Naktong, North to the Yalu: US Army in the Korean War.* Washington: Office of the Chief of Military History, 1986.

Appleman, Roy E. *Korean War.* New York: Gallery Books, 1990.

Berry, Henry. *Hey Mac, Where Ya Been?* New York: St. Martin's Press, 1988.

Blair, Clay. *Beyond Courage.* New York: Ballantine Books, 1955.

Blair, Clay. *A General Life (Omar Bradley).* New York: Simon and Schuster, 1983.

Boettcher, Thomas D. *First Call – The Making of the Modern U.S. Military, 1945-1953.* Boston: Little, Brown & Co., 1992.

Brady, Jim. *The Coldest War.* New York: St. Martin's Griffin, 1990.

Crawford, C. S. *The Four Deuces: A Korean War Story.* Novato, CA: Presidio Press, 1998.

Egeberg, Roger Olaf, M.D. *The General, MacArthur and the Man He Called "Doc".* Washington: Hippocrene Books, 1993.

Fehrenback, T. R. *This Kind of War.* New York: Macmillan, 1963.

Futrell, Robert F. *The United States Air Force History in Korea 1950-1953.* Office of the Air Force History, 1983.

George, Alexander L. *The Chinese Communist Army in Action.* New York: Columbia University Press, 1967.

Giangreco, D. M. *War in Korea 1950-1953.* Novato, CA: Presidio Press, 1990.

Goncharov, Sergei, Lewis, John W., and Litae, Zue. *Uncertain Partners.* Stanford, CA: Stanford University Press, 1994.

Goulden, Joseph. *Korea: The Untold Story of the War.* New York: Times Books, 1982.

Halliday, Jon, and Cumings, Bruce. *Korea, the Unknown War.* New York: Pantheon Books, 1988.

Hastings, Max. *The Korean War.* New York: Simon & Schuster, 1987.

Hermes, Walter G. *Truce Tent and Fighting Front: The US Army in the Korean War.* Washington: Office of the Chief of Military History, US Army, 1988.

Hinshaw, Arned L. *Heartbreak Ridge: Korea 1951.* New York: Praeger Publishers, 1989.

Hopkins, William B. *One Bugle, No Drums: The Marines at Chosin Reservoir.* Chapel Hill, NC: Algonquin Books, 1986.

Hoyt, Edwin P. *The Bloody Road to Panmunjom.* New York: Military Heritage Press, 1985.

———. *The Pusan Perimeter.* New York: Military Heritage Press, 1988.

———. *The Day the Chinese Attacked.* New York: McGraw-Hill, 1990.

Isaacson, Walter, and Evan Thomas. *The Wise Men: Six Friends and the World They Made.* New York: Simon & Schuster, 1986.

Kim, Chum-kon. *The Korean War 1950-1953.* Seoul: Kwangmyong Publishing Company, 1980.

Knox, Donald. *The Korean War: An Oral History-Pusan to Chosin.* San Diego: Harcourt Brace Jovanovich, 1985.

MacDonald, Sallum A. *Korea: The War Before Vietnam.* New York: Macmillan, 1986.

Maihafer, Henry J. *From the Hudson to the Yalu.* College Station, TX: Texas A&M Press, 1993.

Marshall, S.L.A. *Pork Chop Hill – The American Fighting Man in Action- Korea, Spring 1953.* New York: Wm. Morrow & Co., 1956.

———. *Battle at Best.* New York: Wm. Morrow & Co., 1963.

Matloff, Maurice, General Editor. *American Military History.* Washington: Center of Military History, 1969.

Matray, James. *The Reluctant Crusade: American Foreign Policy in Korea 1941-1950.* University of Hawaii Press, 1985.

McCullough, David. *Truman.* New York: Simon & Schuster, 1992.

Mossman, Billy C. *Ebb and Flow: The US Army in the Korean War*. Washington: Center of Military History, 1992.

Paik, Sun Yup. *From Pusan to Panmunjon*. New York: Brassey's (US) Inc., 1992.

Paschall, Rod. *Witness to War, Korea*. New York: Perigee, 1995.

Pratt, Sherman W. *Decisive Battles of the Korean War*. New York: Vantage Press, 1992.

Ridgway, Matthew B. *The Korean War*. New York: Doubleday, 1967.

Russ, Martin. *The Last Parallel*. New York: Kensington, 1957.

Sawyer, Robert K. *KMAG in Peace and War*. Washington: Center of Military History, 1985.

Schnabel, James F. *Policy and Direction- The First Year: US Army in the Korean War*. Washington: Office of the Chief of Military History, US Army, 1972.

Sheldon, Walt. *Hell or High Water: MacArthur's Landing at Incheon*. New York: Ballantine, 1968.

Spurr, Russell. *Enter the Dragon: China's Undeclared War Against the U.S. in Korea, 1950-1951*. New York: Henry Holt, 1988.

Stanton, Shelby L. *America's Tenth Legion: X Corps in Korea, 1950*. Novato, CA: Presidio, 1989.

Stokesbury, James L. *A Short History of the Korean War*. New York: Wm. Morrow & Co., 1988.

Summers, Henry G. Jr. *Korean War Almanac*. New York: Facts on File, 1990.

———. *On Strategy II*. New York: Dell, 1992.

Thornton, Richard C. *China: A Political History 1917–1980*. Boulder: Westview Press, 1982.

Toland, John. *In Mortal Combat*. New York: Wm. Morrow & Co., 1991.

Whelan, Richard. *Drawing the Line*. Boston: Little, Brown & Co., 1990.

Williams, William J., Editor. *A Revolutionary War*. Chicago: Imprint Publications, 1993.

Wilson, Jim. *Retreat Hell!: The Epic Story of the 1st Marines in Korea*. New York: Wm. Morrow & Co., 1988.

ABOUT THE AUTHOR

Kenneth Francis Joseph Santor was born in Buffalo, New York, in 1931, the third of eleven children, and grew up in the era of the Great Depression, which had a great impact on the life of this American Marine. Ken enlisted in the Marines at the age of seventeen, and he eventually served as a machine gunner in Second Section of Charlie Company, First Battalion, First Marines, First Marine Division, under the command of Marine legend, Colonel Chesty Puller and General O. P. Smith at the Frozen Chosin. Charlie Company landed at Incheon on the first wave at Blue Beach, South Korea, and the second wave at Wonsan, North Korea, during 1950–1951, and this is Ken's story of his Korean War experience and his life after surviving what has been called "the Forgotten War."

Printed in the USA
CPSIA information can be obtained
at www.ICGtesting.com
LVHW012042021024
792718LV00017B/188